THE BEAT GOES ON

A Street Cop's Stories

Donna & Dave
Scary isn't it?

[signature]

THOMAS FRIBBS

PAGE PUBLISHING, INC.
New York, NY

First originally published by Page Publishing, Inc. 2018

ISBN 978-1-64350-351-6 (Paperback)
ISBN 978-1-64350-352-3 (Digital)

Printed in the United States of America

THE WARRIOR YEARS

1971–2001

Centurion—in the glorious days of the Roman Empire, the Centurions were the police and warriors, the keepers of order. Society has and always will require a breed of people who will guard the masses sheep from what have been described at times as the *Wolfs*. When there is danger, the *Sheep Dogs* move to intercept and remain till the danger passes. Centurions ran toward the sound of battle; police officers run to the sound of gunfire. Any reasonable person would go the other direction.

While the term *centurion* may have passed since the days of Rome, the lives of your modern Centurions aren't very different.

The following pages contain incidents from the author's years on the street. Enjoy the ride …

INTRODUCTION

I will evoke plausible deniability. Some of the call signs, names, and locations have been changed or altered for my own reasons or more realistically, I just don't remember.

In police work, "street work," be it small-town or large, given a length of time, most kinds of inhumanity to man will cross the officer's path. The larger and more intense the city or area (beat) they cover will yield a more frequent display of this brutality. Police work (real street work) can be likened to war on a smaller scale. Patton said, "Compared to war, all other forms of human endeavor shrink to insignificance." I am not saying police work and war are the same; however, military veterans I worked with often made that comparisons.

To start this journey, I will try to help you understand some of the police talk, jargon, and methods used in the street. My comments are reflective of officers working the street, not to be confused with some of the candy cake, mambzie pambzie, hands-off downtown details. A basic police street squad is the core of all police work. A squad consists of one sergeant and eight to ten officers assigned to cover a geographic area of responsibility. The size, in square miles, is determined by the number of calls for police service recorded for that area. The more calls, the smaller the area the squad can cover.

It works that way for all three shifts: days, afternoons, nights. Add up all the squads and you have a district. The number of districts would reflect the size of the city.

Officer assignments, based usually on their seniority, can rotate in and out of squads and shifts. I did so love it. I would have gladly worked for free if I didn't have bills to pay. To miss working a Friday or Saturday night was unthinkable. Miss the action/fun? Never!

Ah, I had just transferred back to 900 District, feeling comfortable in my soundings. Regular weekend night, around 10:30 p.m., radio chatter was beginning to be nonstop. Took a while to learn how to get your requests answered. A hot tone shrilled the airways. "All units be advised 400 is requesting 906 (officer needs help immediately) Twenty-Fourth Street and Broadway Road." That location, known to all as the most dangerous location in the city of Phoenix, meant serious trouble. I advised en route! With lights and siren, I was soon racing down Twenty-Fourth Street from East Van Buren. The seconds ticked off with units arriving and no Code 4 (no further help needed). Damn, this must be real bad. I crossed the bridge over the Salt River at warp speed, increasing each mph, as still no Code 4. The scene as I approached could best be described as an "action-packed Hollywood blockbuster movie set." Fire trucks, numerous police cars all parked everywhere. Hundreds of people milling around the street and sidewalks. Total chaos. I saw several officers fighting with different groups. Real fistfights and night sticks. Officer Jerry H., who was trading blows with a huge black male, told me to cover his back.

Police units were still arriving with sirens blaring. This was the real deal, no idea what had caused all this. Just wade in and see what happens. A large group began to gather where Jerry was winning his fight, so that was my signal to move in. This crowd of thirty-some was chanting "Get the pig!" as they advanced on me. A real moment of police work had descended on me; how to confront this mob wasn't clear. I was truly afraid but calm at the same time. With my six-cell steel flashlight and MACE spray, one in each hand, I yelled at the advancers, "Come on, you motherfuckers, let's see how many of your skulls I can split." There was a brief pause as the front row evaluated my threat.

Someone yelled out, "That mo' fuck cop crazy." Much to my relief, they were dispersing. Of course, the Calvary was arriving at the same time. Oh, the good old days. "The older I get, the better it was" is the old-timers' saying.

Follow up—the original call for service had come from Fire Rescue, responding to a pedestrian's hit in the crosswalk. Seems the crowd wanted to lynch the driver involved. He had taken refuge in the fire truck. Oh yeah, this driver had been involved in a shooting of an LEO (law enforcement officer) a couple years back.

This is how and why I came to be a police officer:

My police career began somewhat differently. I, unlike many a boy, hadn't given any thought to being a policeman while growing up in my small midwestern town. Cops were to be avoided. I was familiar with a lot of the officers in and around Ottawa, Illinois, my hometown, as most had given me at least one ticket. I wasn't a troublemaker, but trouble managed to find me. Nothing big, just minor scrapes. Sometime around age eighteen, I began to understand my antics, when it came to breaking the law, could become serious and stopped my nonsense.

Graduation, marriage and full time working followed my days of high school. Fortunately, I saw my path as a dead-end street and went back to college to enhance my future. Upon completing my associate degree, I uprooted my little family and moved from the snowy, cold, humid Midwest to the hot, dry deserts of Arizona.

Phoenix, Arizona

I was in my midtwenties when I had my first thoughts of becoming a policeman. It was 1968, and the Democrats were holding their presidential nomination convention in Chicago. This was the same year that Martin Luther King Jr. and Bobby Kennedy were killed. There was a lot of unrest and discontent in the country. President Johnson had us heavily involved in the Vietnam War, and tensions among many college students ran high. The Chicago Police were known for their no-nonsense reputation, and the protesters were out to find out how far they could be pushed. Bags of shit and piss had been thrown at the police lines, and civil disobedience was in the air. Officials had led several legal protest marches down dead-end streets and alleys, etc., causing lots of resentment and confusion. Finally, push came to shove, and Chicago's famous Mayor Richard Daly told the police to disperse the protestors. What followed, per history, were many cracked heads and broken arms and legs. The media, of course, only showed the protestor's injuries. In spite of this, the convention nominated Hubert Humphrey and left town. Following the convention, there was a famous trial involving seven student conspirators. A call for an investigation into what the liberals called "the police riot" also went out.

All of this really is leading up to why I became interested in police work. Former Attorney General Ramsey Clark was named to head up a Blue Ribbon panel on the so-called police riot. After much finger pointing, hand wringing, and *tsk*-ing, this blue ribbon panel's conclusion boiled down to "The police were poorly lead and trained."

Clark summarized by claiming the same element of society produces police officers and criminals. This meant they were generally stupid and unreliable, so why had America expected anything better out of their cops? This really upset me. I thought, *I wouldn't mind being a cop*. They looked good to me. I didn't consider myself stupid, so who was this Clark guy to spout off?

Around 1970, I was working at Motorola and had made a new friend, Jim T. We discussed the idea of becoming police officers. We both felt the same about it being an honorable job. Jim had a friend who was on the Phoenix Police Department, so we went to talk to him. Jim's friend, Officer Ted P., was a patrolman and appeared to be real squared away. He was informative and suggested some things we should consider like rotating shift, loss of friends, etc. Jim and I both had good jobs at Motorola, and it would mean a pay cut for us. We didn't advance past the talking stage at that time. It was several years later when Jim signed up and I tried. As part of the physical entrance exam, I found the vision requirement was twenty-twenty uncorrected. I couldn't pass that. It seemed I was at a dead end.

A side note I had memorized the eye chart in an effort to pass it. Almost succeed till they brought out a different chart for me to read—busted. I opted for the Phoenix Police Reserve, who allowed a person to do all the same functions of a regular officer without pay. Yep, free. My uncorrected vision was okay as long as I was doing it for free. Yeah, that's what I thought. I found the work to be fascinating. I often worked both Friday and Saturday nights. Thus began life's saga for me for the next twenty-five years plus.

CHAPTER 1

Reserve Officer Days, 1972–1975

Reserve officer training was classroom two nights a week and all day Sunday for six months. They said it was equivalent to the regular's academy.

Our uniform was the same as a regular officer with the exception, our badge read "Reserve" on it. The night I graduated from the Reserve Academy, my new training officer, Barry B, suggested we hit the streets since we were already dress for it. He was a stock broker and had been an reserve officer for a few years. I was so nervous, afraid I would screw something up. My first radio call as a reserve was "Monkeys disturbing at a zoo on north Seventh Street." When I snickered my training officer looked real serious and asked me what I thought I was going to do about it. I suggested we stop at a Circle K and get some bananas. We did, problem solved.

I really hoped, each time I went out (Reserve days), I wouldn't do something stupid and embarrass myself. I wasn't afraid of the suspects just my ability to do the job right.

While in the reserves, hoping for the vision requirement to change, I became a sergeant. In that capacity, I was asked to sit on the oral boards for new reserve candidates selection. The Police Reserve unit followed most of the regular police unit's methods for selecting its officers. A three-member supervisor board grilled the prospects.

The assembled candidates were lined up in the hall waiting, following their passing a written test. The point of the oral board was to weed out undesirables and loons. The Oral Board consisted of two reserve and one regular sergeants. While the requirements for reserve officers were not as demanding as the regular officers, we would try to rattle them. I'll give a few examples.

"In the course of your duties, if necessary, would you be able to take the life of another human?"

"No," came an answer from a candidate.

Hum, pressing on. "You have walked up to a door at a family fight. When the door opens, a male shoots your partner. What are you going to do?"

"Oh! I could never shoot someone." *Next.*

Disqualification wasn't usually that automatic as we probed for flaws. Finishing up with one real doofus candidate, I asked, "Do you have any question of us?"

"Yes, how big a gun can I carry?" *Next.* It was interesting to see the parade of wannabes that came through. Even more interesting was some of the ones that got through the testing and training. Had one fellow who used to mow his grass in his full uniform. When confronted, he said it kept his neighbor from sic'ing his dog after him. True story. One, a car salesman in real life joined so he would have first access to folks who had their cars stolen. Mind you, all and all the reserves were a very good group of dedicated people.

Most weekends, I would partner up with a regular officer or another reserve, and out to the streets we went. Years later, I was told the regulars had a lot of respect for us. Rumors began to spread the vision requirement was changing to twenty-twenty corrected. That I could do. I took all the tests, and soon I was at the city doctor's office taking my physical. This was the same office I had visited a few years back and was busted while trying to pass the eye test after memorizing the eye chart.

CHAPTER 2

Waiting to Report to the Academy

I was given a February 1975 appointment date for the academy and prepared to shut down my career at Motorola. My boss, Dennis P., had been a reserve officer back in New York State and was all for my change. I was real excited about this change and had all the family's support. I was getting ready to turn in my notice at my job when we were informed due to the federal government supplying so much equipment to the police department, a stipulation was issued requiring all new recruits be selected from persons who had been unemployed for at least two months. My source at the department didn't know when a regular hired academy would start. What a letdown. The summer of 1975 was a long one indeed. At Motorola, I had chummed up with another reserve officer, Jim W. Reserve officers were only allowed to ride with a regular officer or a certified reserve car commander.

Jimmy W was my reserve car commander. We both worked at Motorola and hit it off real well. Getting a good partner is the first order of business. Our families had cookouts and went camping around the state. Jimmy was the production manager for the Motorola plant, he was looking at a serious pay cut to go regular, so he was staying put. Late in 1975, I got the word an academy for regular hires would start in November. This was to be the only class that year. Being a reserve, I was mentally prepared and physically ready to go. The word from the academy was many of the unemployed type were worthless, so there was a major effort to get recruits to quit during the academy training. Thus the staff was employing major stress, both mental and physical, as a means to accomplish that task.

I stepped up my running and weight training. On a Sunday, one week before my Academy start date, I was at the academy for a reserve meeting and decided to see how my time on the obstacle course had improved. Off I ran, tearing it up. Up, over, and through the course I ran. I turned the corner for the home stretch, which was downhill. I was cooking as I crossed the finish line and stepped in a depression. I turned my ankle completely over. Oh no, what had I done? The emergency room doctor stared at me when I explained I had to be ready to run in a week. He said maybe I could put some weight on my ankle in a week; there wouldn't be any running. Well, he had his timetable and I had mine. It wasn't broken, so I was giving a plastic cast to wrap it and told to stay off it.

Two-a-day runs and lots of boot camp yelling is what the staff was into. I didn't know what to do. I wasn't missing my chance at the academy, and I had already quit my job at Motorola. I heard if I got through the orientation they would recycle me putting me to work downtown doing something till a new class was formed. Who knew when that would be? I was somehow going to make it, period. I was walking painfully on it by Tuesday. Orientation was on Wednesday at the main police station. To hide my limping on my damaged ankle, I got to the office early. We were busy filling out paperwork, insurance forms, etc. All was going fine when the fire alarm went off. Captain Smith, a friend, was conducting the process and noticed me limping as we exited the building. He was not pleased with me as I showed him the walking cast. "You were planning to start on Monday with that ankle?"

"Yep, that was my plan."

We talked about desire and guts and such, and he said reluctantly, "Well, go ahead. We'll see what happens."

Monday morning was looming and I was very nervous. The scene was set. I truly could hardly put any weight on my ankle. Running would probably make me pass out, but I would get through it somehow.

CHAPTER 3

Reporting to the Academy

Monday morning, November 17, 1975, came early. I was driving below the speed limit as I approach the academy. I knew they set speed traps for recruits to begin altering their civilian behavior. I was flagged to a stop by Sergeant Dave T., a friend, and told to surrender my driver's license. My protest I wasn't speeding went unanswered, and I continued on to find a parking place.

My life would never be the same!

Our ragtag group of about forty recruits were sitting at desks in building 3. Each desk had a paper name tag looking like a little pup tent on it and a large envelope. It was all foreign to most. The Class Sergeant, Jim G. from Tempe, along with other sergeants, lieutenants, and staff crashed into the room, announcing, "Good morning, class."

We weakly replied, "Good morning." That was the last civil thing I heard for many weeks.

The yelling started. "Get your PT [physical training] gear on and assemble on the parade ground. Now! Now! Now! Move it! Move it! Move it!" Holy crap, I wasn't ready for this. Recruits were tripping over each other.

"Where and what is the parade ground?" someone asked. The counselors and staff were in the locker rooms, yelling and causing more confusion. It was awful. Somehow, the confused group made it to the parade ground for stretching exercise prior to going on our first run. My swollen ankle was numb by now, and I figured I would pass out soon to end the misery.

I felt Ralph G., an officer I knew from my reserve days, come alongside me asking, "How's the ankle?"

I replied it was still sore, and he went off on me.

"Don't you know how to address the staff? *Sir!* will proceed everything out of your mouth, you worthless piece of crap," and on and on. He then chewed me out for being in the exercising area in the first place. "If you further injure that ankle, we will have your ass," etc. I guessed someone had told the staff I was not allowed to run on it until it was better. I wish I had been told. He told me to go to the weight room and work out while the class was on the run. There were many of the assembled recruits giving me the stink eye as they ran off without me. I went to the weight room as directed. I looked the place over, checking for hidden cameras. I was lifting weights at the time, so I thought my routine would work fine. I pressed for max weight and had worked up a good sweat when my class with the counselors returned. For the most part, the class was hurting, coughing, spitting, and a few upchucking.

Mind you, we had about fifteen staff members all trying to get your attention by threats of reprisals for your lack of performance. "Get down to the range for physical training *now!*" I was told my ankle wouldn't be a problem exercising, "so get with your class, you slacker." This new entertainment was designed to improve your strength and stamina, we were being told.

Push-ups, leg lifts, squat-thrusts, etc. were demonstrated by first one counselor, then a new one would take over, followed by the class doing the exercise to a count. If you have ever lifted weights, you know after finishing your sets, your arm might as well be noodles. I couldn't do a full push-up if my life depended on it. I was pathetic. The staff was milling around, yelling and cursing anyone who wasn't keeping up. They, of course, were each doing only one exercise then trading off with another staff for the next one. I will always remember hearing how they were doing everything they were asking of us, yeah right. Throwing up wasn't allowed on the range; you had to ask for permission to leave the area to barf. The terror ended with a call to shower and get to class in five minutes. Punishment was promised for any person tardy. The counselors even followed us into the showers and locker rooms. It was going to be a long day.

We were back in the classroom, where the harassment continued with a self-evaluation quiz taking place. Each recruit was asked to tell a little about themselves and why they wanted to be a police officer. The staff stood around, snickering to themselves at our feeble attempts to explain our motives. The day was a blur with homework assignments and new issued gear. The gear was to be polished and the written assignments done by tomorrow at roll call. No excuses—errors would not be allowed. I headed for home, wondering what I had done to myself. I was thirty-three years old and had a nice home and family. What was I doing? Supper was a salad as my stomach was flipping and my mind was on fire. How would I get everything done and sleep? Well, I didn't sleep the first night. Not at all, but I was ready in the morning to face the staff with my gear and written assignments in order.

Day two was a carbon copy of the first day except my time in the weight room was spent stretching only, not lifting. I was good to go when the bedraggled class returned from the run. We were off to the exercising arena, where my apparent metamorphosis seemed to impress the staff. I was hitting each set of exercises with no issue. My overnight transformation was amazing indeed. My councilor was impressed with my improvement and told me so, never knowing the truth. Our homework assignments were wrong, of course, the red marks reflecting such. Now the trick was correct and rewrite them along with a new longer assignment for tonight's project. Why? Well, since we had screwed our first assignment, we needed more practice. This pattern continued till the end of the week. Though I had been excused from running the first week, the exercising was grueling on my ankle. The swelling never went down, and I should have taken out stock with Bayer Aspirin Company. It was really hurting. On Friday of the first week, my councilor sent me to the city doctor to determine if I would be okay to run with the class the second week. The doctor asked me what I thought. Knowing I was facing recycling, with no known date for a new class to form, I told him it was just fine. I had the whole weekend to rest it.

Monday morning came around way too soon. We dressed out to the screams of the staff and anyone else hanging around. We were imbeciles, incapable of function without their yelling and threats. The stretching exercises went okay as the moment of truth approached. "Lines of two ready! Begin!" and off we went. I ran at least three steps before I stepped on a pebble the size of a boulder (really maybe a very small rock). The pain shot up my leg, and I saw white. Run or pull up lame—a huge decision had to be made right there and then. I guess I figured I would pass out before it killed me, so on I ran. The pain became a dull throb as I stayed up with the group midway along the strung-out class. This became my position for the next few weeks. This group was really out of shape, and I didn't stand out by hanging back with them. The ankle never healed due to the running, but I did learn to tolerate the pain, and soon enough, I was running up with the front of the class. I can't say I enjoyed PT, but I had no problem with it.

We were being mentally and physically reconditioned from civilians to police officers. In the civilian world, okay was good enough, but not here. I was able to get a few hours of sleep each night and, refreshed, charged forward. A pattern began to form, where the weak were singled out for extra attention. It soon was apparent keeping your mouth shut and only speaking when spoken to was the clue to easier times. We were dropping recruits right and left. Ten to twelve the first week. The attrition continued at a few a week for a while till we were down to twenty. It was mystifying to me how after going through the hell of the first week, you would give up. I had chummed up with another recruit, Bruce A., who was closer to my age of thirty-three. The rest of the recruits had broken up into little clicks. The trouble was the dumb were hanging out with the dumb, so they were told to split up and study with the smarter recruits. It was a refresher course for me since as a reserve officer, I had received all of the same training. I was looking forward to our two weeks in the street for OJT (on-the-job training). I was sent to 700 Squaw

Peak District for my stint. It was great. Officer Bob B. was my training officer and couldn't believe how ready for the street I was.

Too soon we were back at the academy but looking forward to graduation. We received our district assignments. Mine was 700 District. I had hoped for 900 District, where I had spent three years as a reserve. Another recruit assigned to 900 asked if I wanted to swap our assignments. I agreed. The problem was I didn't know he hadn't cleared it with the staff. I was called in and told if I didn't like my assignment, I could resign and hit the trail. Wow, did they rake me over. I made a feeble attempt to excuse my stupidity and was told to get out of the office. I had made the mistake of thinking I had a mind of my own and learned I still didn't. I did let the other recruit know how stupid he was. A thought continued to run through my head all during the academy. If we were being prepared to go out into the streets and take control, facing all kinds of dangers, why were they treating us like helpless little children? We virtually weren't to do anything without permission and felt the wrath of at least a councilor if tried. There seemed to be a consorted attempt to embarrass the recruits, often, holding someone up to the class as a poor example by lecturing or showing them up on some task. Now mind you, the person had committed some infraction, but the other recruits hadn't, so why show us what we didn't do wrong? It was confusing. I had the advantage of having worked the streets already in the reserves, so I knew what was to be expected. Bruce and I discussed this situation on several occasions. Our consensus was it would pass, and when we graduated we'd forget about it. Graduation day was approaching, and I was so ready to get out of there.

I was only selected once to participate in field problems at the academy. The set-up was while on patrol, you enter a convenience market and find a armed robbery in progress. The two bandits are holding the clerk at gunpoint and demand you drop your gun. They tell you to draw out your gun using your left hand. I complied and shot both of them with that same left hand. The actors, two of our councilors, were embarrassed and made me do it again. This time, they shot me as I came in the door. Now that was some good training, huh? I was left pretty much alone, as the staff knew I had about three years' experience. Remembering back, they did embarrass me during our first day orientation class. They were asking each recruit to tell a little about themselves and any law enforcement experience they had. My turn came, and I advised of my three years with the reserves. The councilor stopped me cold, saying he was asking about "real police work." I knew then and there to keep my mouth shut unless asked a question. Graduation was nice, with counselors and staff talking to you like you were an adult. I didn't trust them though, expecting them to launch into a tirade any moment.

CHAPTER 4

Graduation: Report to the Street

I reported to my assignment, District 700 Squaw Peak Station. Our district's boundaries were I-17 West to Glendale City. Camelback Road north to Dunlap Avenue. Mostly working-class folks. I knew the station's layout and where briefing would be held, having worked out of there as a reserve. Many years back, as a fresh new reserve, I learned when entering a briefing room to wait till the regulars were seated before sitting down. An old cigar-smoking veteran whose seat I had occupied had roundly advised me of that. Yes, there was an unwritten seating order in every briefing I ever attended. My training officer was introduced to me; Officer Ivan S. was to be my mentor. I was to be his first rookie, and he was taking it very seriously. Briefing completed, we spilled out to the hallway to get a patrol car and hit the bricks. Ivan presented me a paper that listed all functions of a police officer's day. He wanted me to rate myself from 1 to 10 on my strengths in each area. I marked 10 on all but traffic accident investigation. He was real confused at this. We didn't do accidents as reserves. I had to explain I had been working two nights a week in the hottest district in Phoenix for the last three years. He had been told I had no experience. He wanted so to be a teacher and I didn't need it. I did manage on our first night to get him his first ever complaint as a police officer.

We had stopped at a convince market for a coffee when a young girl approached and was complaining about someone stealing her cat.

The location of the alleged incident was out of our district, but Ivan wanted to investigate anyway. What, I asked, was to investigate? Cats roam, don't they? She didn't like my answer or my questioning her if she had been smoking dope. To think this was a police matter. I flashed my light in her eyes just to check for dilated pupils and went along with Ivan to her trailer park to "investigate." Ivan went around, talking to neighbors about her drama. I couldn't believe it. Of course, the creature was back home when Ivan thought to check. I was vocal and told him what a waste of time it had been. He was trying his best to sell some PR to me, but I wasn't buying. We went onto other things and got a radio call to meet our sarge. I assumed he wanted to talk to or about me. Wrong, we had gotten a complaint. The husband of the "My cat is missing" girl, upon hearing of my lack of compassion for her plight, had called to complain. Ivan was really upset. The sarge told him complaints were part of doing the job and we hadn't done anything wrong. He sulked the rest of the night. I only rode with him for a short time since I was already more experienced than he was. Soon I was solo and ready to work on my own.

I was partnered up working the paddy wagon on the afternoon shift. Our unit was a standard bread truck–looking utility van painted tan and white with "Phoenix Police" decals. A car in front of us was weaving, so we turned on the overhead lights to pull it over; the offender pulled to the curb. As I approached the car, it drove off. Oh yeah, we quickly got behind it again lit it up and it pulled to the curb again. I opened my door, and off it drove again. That was enough! We sped after the car and pulled in front of it, forcing it to the curb. To my surprise, a little old lady was behind the wheel, looking startled. I motioned for her to roll down her window as I approached. She did and asked, "What is the problem, Officer?"

I questioned her why she kept driving off after I tried to stop her.

"Oh, was that you? I thought you were an ambulance." Huh. Have a nice day!

Rookies are often selected to conduct morbid and really discussing details. "721 Adam, see the detective blah blah location." Now what! A little insider background info is in order: Detectives have no need to talk to uniforms cause they were so much brighter, smarter, and better-looking than street cops. You get the picture. Knowing this, my alert levels were up. Found my requesting detective, an old—and I mean old—salt in a rundown trailer park. This guy had more time in the shitter at 17 S. Second Avenue (police headquarters) than I had on the street.

"Had any dead bodies, kid?"

"Yeah, a few," I said, lying.

"Well, come with me and learn." He paused, lit a big old cigar and puffed on it. (We weren't to be seen smoking in the public.) Wow, this guy was salty.

Into a very rundown trailer we went, with me nearly gagging from the smell inside. If you have had the never-to-be-forgotten experience of smelling a decaying dead body, you understand. If you haven't experienced this, pass on it. It was gas-mask-requirement level. The "Never let them see you sweat" thought went through my mind as I pretended it was no big deal. In the little trailer, a huge form was laying on its back in the only bedroom. I say that because there was no way to determine if the form was male, female, white, black, young, or old. It had exploded; skin was hanging from the arms, legs, and torso. The form looked to be about three hundred pounds and was blackened. Detective "Salty" guessed it had died at least couple of days before and lain there in the one-hundred-plus temperature unnoticed. The stink would have started within a day, so how come no one reported it? Actually, the general area stunk, so I guess this only increased the putrid level. Standing alongside the mass on the bed, my mentor made some general small talk about dead bodies and proper investigating methods while puffing on his cigar, all of which could have been discussed outside of the zone of putrid, decaying flesh. I stayed there with him until he must have grossed himself out, and we left the trailer. He was impressed I'd worked through this test without complaint. Little did he know when I left the call, I drove to my house and took a shower. Washed my hair, cleaning my nostrils with Q-tips. Nothing helped get rid that awful smell. Believe me when I say nothing gets rid of that smell except time.

A story about that most glamorous police activity, kicking in doors. The shift had been routine when I just finished up taking a burglary report for a nice family. I bid them goodbye with my ever-so-professional bearing and walked out to my freshly washed police car. Preparing to leave, I climbed in and switched on the ignition. *Whaaaaa waillllllll whaaaaaa* shattered the silence of the neighborhood. I immediately turned off my siren that had mysteriously been turned to the "on" position. My image was shattered as I slinked away embarrassed. It was a trick played on rookies, and I should have been prepared for it. Old salts and other miscreants from your squad would grab the extra set of keys for your cruiser. While you were away from it or distracted, they would open your door, set the siren to "on" position, and slither away. The siren didn't work while the ignition switch was in the "off" position.

I drove to a secluded spot as the sun was sinking to write my 459 (burglary) report. Two of the siren strikers cruised by, acting innocent of course. It was soon dark, and the radio activity was picking up. I continued to work on my report, since I had been instructed by my sergeant not to let paperwork pile up, the silence was shattered by *beeeeeeeeeeeeeeee* (hot tone). "Any unit in the area of blah-blah location, we have a burglary in progress with a twelve-year-old female home alone." That was *big*. I tossed my routine paperwork to the side, advised radio I was rolling, and sped Code 3 to the scene. En route, no other units had responded, and I was soon 10-23 (arrived). Prior to nearing the location, I had shut off my siren to keep the suspect from hearing me. Lights off, I exited my cruiser and hurried to the house. Radio was advising the twelve-year-old was saying the suspect was trying to enter through a window at the rear of the house. Running through the carport, I saw the house entrance door's window screen was partially torn. I cleared the backyard visually and was now hearing the girl inside screaming for help. Radio and I, yelling from the outside, tried to convince her it was me outside and let me in. She wouldn't. As she screamed "Please someone help me," my size 12 Justin spit-shined boot smashed through the double-dead-bolted front door. Trim, frame, and hardware flew like an explosion from the impact. I charged through the door missing only my cape, to find the teenager minus one year lying on the couch, clutching her teddy bear and the phone. No bad guy, hmmmmmmm. I quickly checked the interior as she couldn't speak. All clear. I declared a code 4 (no further assistance needed). Radio said her parents were en route while I was able to calm her enough to get the story. In fact, someone had been outside trying to break in, as witnessed by several torn screens. No entry had been made, and the pleas I heard her making were to the radio operator, which wasn't relayed to me. The parents arrived and surveyed their shattered front door and, to my relief, understood the need for my dynamic entry. My sergeant, now on the scene, was told they would get the damage repaired on their own. They were so relieved I had saved their daughter from the Bogeyman.

Looking back, I wouldn't have done things differently. Returning to the station, at the end of shift, I thought my night's big drama hot tone response and door kick would be the talk of the station. No, it was the look on my face when my sabotaged siren went off. It was the highlight of the night for most of the officers. So much for the caped crusader.

When I went to work for the Phoenix Police Department. Jimmy stayed working at Motorola, so we kind of lost touch. He would ride with me sometimes, but I was being held as a POW (prisoner of war) against my will in 700 District. 700, compared to 900, was tame. A year or so into my career as a regular, Jimmy called me one day and announced that he too was joining the Phoenix Police Department full time. This was about a 50 percent pay cut for him. The job gets in your blood. There is a thirst that can only be quenched with full-time police work. Corny but true. I watched closely as he headed for the academy since I had had such an awful time there. He went through without a hitch. He seemed to really enjoy himself. He drew 900 District for his assignment, where I was not assigned. It took another year after I completed my transfer from District 700 to 900 before were partners again. We would be working Shift 3 out of old Sky Harbor Station.

THOMAS FRIBBS

A routine call of a runaway brought me to their door. Introductions over, we got down to business. I was already experiencing my own issue with this at home, so enlightened, we pressed forward. "When did you last see her? Has she run away before? How long has she been gone?" The responses you could almost answer for them but were necessary to ask. This was their first experience with a teenaged daughter gone bad. Her very cute fourteen-year-old picture was given to me with a very sincere "Please find her for us."

"I will do my best," I replied. I checked with my supervisor for extra time to work on my new role of kid -finder guy. I think he winked as he sent me off with a "Good luck."

I had been on patrol long enough to know some of the kid hangouts, so I went in search of my sweet little missing runaway. At the park, the kids were less than helpful till one girl said they were at an address on Larkspur where all the creeps hung out. New mission at hand, I headed for the location parking a block away. There was still plenty of light as I approached the unoccupied front poach. The door was open, revealing scattered mattresses, junk food wrappers, pizza boxes, and old magazines on the floor. I walked inside, all 6 feet, 200 pounds of brass shined and polished boots, to a room full of "they couldn't care less" teenagers. My visions of trying to broadcast APBs on all the running youths was burst.

"Oh, hi, Officer, is something wrong?"

Wrong? Wrong, really? Half a dozen preteens hanging around a flop house with no adult supervision—let's think of how many things could go wrong. I spotted my quarry, Emily. I first told her to stay put then approached, waiting for her to rabbit. Didn't happen. "Let's go" was my order.

"Okay," was the short reply.

I was prepared to lecture her on all sorts of the evils on the street; instead, I just took her back to her folks' house a few miles away.

As I arrived with her, they seemed relieved but hesitant. Was I reading too much into this encounter? They wanted to know what she thought she was doing. "How dare you scare your Mother!" the berating began. I tried to excuse myself but was requested to stay to help sort out this difficult scene. I had no original answers. Kids had been running away from home for centuries (one of mine had only a few years back). I did know yelling at them wasn't the answer and told them so.

That brought out "Well, so am I to just let her do as she pleases?" Frustration can bring out the worst in people, and this discussion was going nowhere, so after suggesting the services of a professional, I bid adieu.

I talked to my sergeant, who cautioned about getting too involved in these family issues. A week later, radio advised me to respond to a familiar address on request of the complainant. Hmmm.

Of course Emily was missing again. I asked what had been done about the problem since last we were together. Blank faces greeted me. All the time, Mother had little to say and wouldn't say much today. This was frustrating as it didn't appear anything had been done to alter the situation, so why were they expecting different results?

I agreed to try to find her again and did an hour later. She was squatting with some other kids who swore they were adults until I presented them with contributing to delinquency of a minor. By this time, my squad was pissed at me 'cause every time I found Emily, the kids with or around her also had to be returned to their homes which tied up several squads. My concern wasn't universally felt. Same show back home—yelling threats, etc.

A few weeks went by with no sight of her or activity at the flop house. My curiosity up, I stopped at her house and was met by a very cold mother, who curtly advised me, "Emily is in the custody of the state mental hospital. Her father had her admitted as an incorrigible."

Wow, that took me back. I left and tried imagining the level of parental disappointment necessary to reach that point. Turning your child over to the state—ouch.

Later that week, a phone message was in my office mailbox. "To Officer Fribbs: please call listed number regarding Emily." The number was to the Arizona State Mental Hospital. Several holds later, I was put through to Emily's case worker. We had a brief conversation about the kid. The case worker said Emily had made a request I visit her.

This was way out of my wheelhouse, but I agreed to go if it would help. Arizona State Mental Hospital, try rolling that around in your mind as you pass into the facility. Guards who looked like they would prefer to be anywhere else at every door. Several trusties who reminded you of Igor from the movies. Once inside the waiting room, its name was correct. Fifteen minutes passed as I was about to leave when she came out from a door. She looked fine, even smiling. We made small talk about her dad's decision to commit her. I couldn't break through her shield. It gave me great concern she was seemingly content in this environment. A voice out of an unseen speaker announced, "Attention! Visiting hours are over. All patients return to your facility." I truly was in a prisoner lockdown; it felt bad. I was really confused and concerned as she walked away.

She turned to another girl her age who had asked her who I was. "Oh, he's a pig that I know."

The reality of it all crashed down around my ears. I walked out of there in a mental fog. *"A pig that I know"*?

My "never let them know what your think" shield went up. I learned a valuable lesson about getting too involved in situations you don't have control over. Lesson filed away, I went on with my career.

A normal night's work might be a family fight, a car wreck, and a few noise complaints. Lots of burglary reports as folk would get home from work during our working hours. Too soon I was being transferred to shift 3. I had been solo for some time and really didn't want to work graveyards. I was told I needed the experience. I can't say when it happened, but I fell in love with shift 3. I was having a ball. The real reasons for having a police department are found on third shift. The drunks, the thieves, the derelicts, and the assholes of the world seemed to only come out after midnight. This was what I was made for. I had two new officer friends, Rich W. and Dennis J. They were like me, and we had a great time racing from call to call. I was settling into this life when I got a call from District 900 with a chance to transfer to that hub of action. My days of dealing with too many nonsense calls were soon to be over.

Oh, you think there are no nonsense calls? I'll illustrate a few. Lady called in, wanted me to make the kids stop playing ball in their cul-de-sac street. No! Complaint followed. Lady complained her neighbor's swamp cooler's water was running into her yard. I do not lie. I walked out into the yard, picked up the hose, and threw it back a ways into the offender's yard. I asked her if she had ever thought to do that. Complaint followed. Two businessmen on Bethany Home Road got into a fistfight over where the dirt swept up from their adjoining parking lots should be deposited. I kid you not. One owner had swept it up and dumped in front of the other's front door. I told them to stop acting like eight-year-old kids and grow up. Complaint followed. The final straw was dealing with a huge wreck that occurred at an auto dealership off Forty-Third Avenue. A drunk fell asleep while southbound approaching Glendale. He hit about five cars parked in the lot and knocked down three light poles. Massive damage at 3:00 a.m. No one was at the dealership, so I located an "In the event of an emergency ..." sign. I didn't want to leave the mess for day shift, so I called the number. I got the owner, who asked what I thought *he* could do about it at 3:00 a.m. Talk about pissing me off.

While being held a POW in 700 District the winter of 1976, my sergeant gave me a gift certificate for twenty-five dollars. These little gems were supplied by some insurance institute to reward safe drivers during the holiday season. "Cool," you say. I couldn't find one. Issued lots of tickets for bad driving, but that good driver eluded me. The reward was to be given out by midnight, Christmas Eve. On the twenty-fourth, with the clock ticking, I still had no candidate in sight. Sergeant had told me, "Get rid of it, period." It seemed there was a lot of trouble to return them. My search began in earnest, watching for the slightest model driver. Bingo, a young female driver passed westbound on Bethany Home from Thirty-Fifth Avenue driving at or slightly below the posted speed limit. *Good start*, I thought as I followed from a distance. Down the road we traveled, with her turning on her turn signal for a right-bound north turn at Forty-First Avenue. That's it—she passed the test. I lit her up, smiling to myself, thinking about how thankful she was about to become. I walked up to her car, kinda full of myself, chuckling at my surprise. "License, please."

"Umm, I don't have one, Officer."

Aww geeez, really? She was only fifteen and a half, not even old enough for a permit. She explained her extra careful driving was to avoid being stopped by me.

I explained the reason for the stop, laughing at the outcome. She was less than a block from her home. I gave her the check anyway, advising her to leave my name out of any story she told about this encounter. Squaw Peak Station (700) was very typical of most precincts in large cities. Nice homes where most people will have little to no contact with their police department.

My issue was I had learned my trade at Sky Harbor Station (900). That was where the action was, and I wanted back. I'll admit the silly complaints by those nice folks in 700 may have hastened my decision.

CHAPTER 5

Goodbye to 700 Squaw Peak

Released from 700 District for good (or maybe bad) behavior. I bid farewell to the Squaw Peak Station and headed south to then 900 Sky Harbor Station. I was welcomed by a few of the old regulars I had worked with while in the reserves. It felt good. My new sergeant, Steve S., was the current state power lifting champion and looked to be an ass kicker. He assigned me to the least active beat at the eastern edge of the district that abutted Tempe. I guessed he wanted to see how I would react to working 900 District.

The calls for service began immediately. Man with a gun, shots fired, subject down and bleeding, etc. I raced into the heart of the squad area each time but too late to take charge. I was at the scene of a man down whose head was pouring blood. This would have been big in 700. Sergeant took me aside and asked me what was I doing there. I tried to make it seem I was needed. He explained unless officers were fighting suspects or needed to round up witnesses, we usually handled these types of calls with one officer. He was trying to tell me to stay out in my area where nothing was happening. The night wore on, and he caught me a couple more times responding to calls out of my area. We finally agreed if I wasn't going to stay out in my assigned area, he might as well move me in to a beat where the action was. I think I passed his test wondering if I would want to be involved in the action. I was back home and loved it.

CHAPTER 6

Home at Last

This was my old haunt, East Van Buren. The shootings, cuttings, stabbings, whores, bar fights, and drunks with the Duce, Projects, and Barrio thrown in. It was a policeman's Mecca. I had worked it as a reserve and wanted back in the real action. The first shift back after N Days (nonwork days) was Friday, and we started about 10:00 p.m. Every night was gangbusters. We would be running from call to call until an arrest was made. If you were partnered up, one guy wrote the reports and necessary paperwork for booking as we drove to the jail. You simply didn't want to miss the action. Officers who went to the station with their prisoners to do paperwork were not thought too highly of. There existed an unwritten competition between the squads for arrest numbers. This could cause the sergeant to hunt down arrests for the squad to do. We hated this and often told them, "You caught it, you clean it." They didn't, of course, as they were always needed for more important things. We had a real pride in our squad area and our ability to kick ass and take names.

The real point of most of our efforts was to provide safety to us. I'll explain. When we located a bar, restaurant, dance hall, etc., that was not paying proper respect to the police, we went about correcting this issue. Let's say an officer had to fight with patrons to affect an arrest at one of these places. This meant the locals would have to be reminded who was in charge. A few nights of arresting anyone who even looked cross-eyed usually took care of any future problems. There was a bar called El Calderon's Copper State Buffet. Totally Mexicans and always jumping. The bouncer for the joint, Russell C, was fair sized and was very quick to use his nightstick to solve a problem. We had to explain to Russell if a trip to the hospital for stitches following his arrests was his result, we didn't want to be called. He complied by seeing his contacts were carted off somewhere to heal. One night, after an officer had to call for backups, war was declared on the El Calderon. We made the place a project. If you weren't on a call, you made passes through its parking lot, and anything slightly wrong went to jail or got cited. It only took about two weekends before the locals would hold the door open for you when it was necessary to go to the El Calderon. All people understand force and respect power when they know they are in the wrong. We worked hard and never turned away from a fight. The police officers of that time had the backing of their sergeants and lieutenants and went about the business of keeping a lid on the city. A saying back then was "If you aren't getting complaints, you must not be doing much." Today that has changed to "If you are getting complaints, where there is smoke, there must be fire."

CHAPTER 7

A Picture of East Van Buren Street, Phoenix, Arizona Late Seventies

To the unaware, I will attempt to paint a picture of East Van Buren [EVB] Street during the 1970s to 1980s.

Named for Martin Van Buren, this presidential-named street held no resemblance to that great American. EVB stretched the better part of ten miles through the heart of the great city of Phoenix, Arizona. In earlier years, it was a main thoroughfare through the city connecting Phoenix, with Tempe and Mesa to the east. The western edge took you out to the country and farmland beyond. When I moved to Phoenix in 1966, it was well on its way to establishing its sorted reputation. Nothing was off limits on EVB. Originally, fine motels lined each side of the street. The proximity to Sky Harbor Airport and Arizona State University made it popular with travelers.

Prostitution sums up the EVB story. Why the decline and decadence over the years? I have no idea. When I started in the Police Reserves around 1971, the city's East Van Buren area was well into its fall from greatness. Prostitutes walked the streets, with some boldly standing on every corner. Johns, trying to make their selection, cruised back and forth, making for a small parade. Did the city fathers condone this in-your-face display of criminal activity? We were tacitly advised there were more important issues to be dealt with than these victimless crimes. Really!

Let's talk about some of these victimless crimes, shall we?

Every—without exception, every—girl I ever dealt with on EVB was hooked on drugs. All showed tracks (collapsed veins from injecting dope) along with rotting teeth and open sores. They didn't start out that way, but only about a year was necessary to achieve that result. A new girl would appear on the street. She was usually from out of state, and most came here because of the mild weather. We would question her, "Who are you working for?" "Myself" was the usual answer. Often by the end of the week, maybe sooner, she would be at the County Hospital Emergency Room (ER) with injuries. Either one of the black pimps or one of the older established girls would find issues with her "working for herself." The injuries would range from a beating to the body (pimp administered) can't damage the appearance for further earnings to serious cuttings requiring stitches. If another whore had gotten to her, broken bones were certain. Territorial issues. It was not unusual for twenty to twenty-five girls to be out walking EVB. The johns would be prowling, and around 11:00 p.m., the calls for robbery and thieves would start. Here is a typical incident:

"What can I do for you, sir?"

"My wallet was stolen."

"I see, any idea how that happened?"

"No, it's just gone."

"Well, I will need a few more details, like your name, address, phone number, etc."

"Why?"

"If you intend to make a report, we will have to investigate."

"You can't call me or come to my house."

"Why is that?"

"Never mind, you won't find it anyway."

And so it went, night after night. John picked up the girl; while he had his pants down and enjoyed his moment of pleasure, she stole his money, credit cards, wallet—anything available. He couldn't stop her cause he couldn't follow with his drawers around his ankles. Victimless crimes, right? Teenager girls, some as young as twelve, often runaways, would appear on the streets. They lied about their age and circumstances, defying you to prove otherwise.

If you did break down their story, usually they had come in on the Dog (Greyhound Bus), where the pimps lurked in the shadows, waiting to befriend this lost child. We did, on occasion, return them to their very worried family out of state. Youth stolen, victimless crimes? How many broken marriages resulting from diseases brought home were never reported?

Territorial disputes often came to our attention. I was cruising EVB when my attention was drawn to a scuffle on the sidewalk. Nothing big, two whores fighting. I pulled into the divider lane and started to exit my car when my eye caught the flash of steel as I now saw the two prostitutes fighting with blades. One had a straight razor (barber-style) while her nemesis had a four-inch buck knife. Razor Girl was cut from her right eye to below her chin with the skin flapping loose. She was now on the bottom, and Buck Knife Girl was arcing the knife down to finish stabbing Razor. Holy crap, right in front of me. I yelled in my loudest, deepest, and most authoritative voice, "Put down the knife or I'll blow your fucking head off." In midair, she threw the knife as Razor Girl also dropped her blade. Was I good? Jimmy arrived in another unit, and we took stock of the situation.

Razor had two visible cuts, both about six inches long, to her face and neck. Buck Knife had similar cuts to her face. Both were gushing blood from the open wounds. Disarmed, we led them to our cars for transportation, as they would bleed out waiting for fire rescue on a Saturday night. Without a spoken word, we put one in each car and drove Code 3 to County Hospital one half mile away. I had given each rolls of gauss to help stop the bleeding. We marched them into County Hospital's very chaotic ER area. I stopped the head nurse, a friend, and quickly told her we had two bleeding out. Her response was, "What do you want me to do? I have two gunshot victims dying on me and a house full of fucked-up people. Oh, never mind. We'll see if we can stop the blood till you can get to them, okay?"

"Fine, you know where stuff is." We found two empty rooms while picking up dressings on the way. The girls were crying and apologizing to each other, so we settled on one room. We stopped the bleeding, cleaned them up as best as we knew how. Later, after the crisis with the gunshot victims was over (both died), the nurses took over. Neither girl wanted to press charges, as it was all a misunderstanding about their pimp. Jimmy and I went to our police station to wash the blood out of the cars and went 10-8 (back in service). Victimless crimes?

No weekend night went by without overdoses, stabbings, and the occasional murder. They were all related to the prostitution on EVB. Every so often, orders from downtown would come down: "Clean up EVB." Maybe a VIP's folks had flown in and saw the human blight as they came out from Sky Harbor Airport passing through EVB. Never knew what spurred the crackdowns. First, a sting operation would be planned. This involved putting one or two female undercover officers out on the street to entice the johns. Sounds like entrapment, ya? Actual entrapment involved getting a person to do something they weren't prepossessed to do. English ... the john had to solicit the undercover officer for a sex act with a price. The logistics involved a couple of motorcycle officers for chasing down a drive-away, a couple of marked cars for the takedown, a video van, and a command van for processing the suspects. Yes, this was quite an effort. The first thing that happened, the local whores took the night off and went home, knowing the undercover girls (usually quite good-looking) would get all the business. Here we go! Everyone was in place as the female officer walked out to the sidewalk to immediately be hit on by a passing motorist. Once he told her what he wanted and how much he would pay, she would pull her ear or other signal and the john's life turned upside down. Flashing lights, big black-booted police officers jerking him out of his car, handcuffs clicked, and a walk down to the processing van. All suspects were booked into jail to enhance the effect.

The street takedown took about two minutes, and the scene was clear for the next unlucky horny fool. The female officer's conversation had been taped, so she wasn't in need for processing the schmuck. This would go on for only a couple of hours 'cause the paperwork would soon back up the process. One night during a sting, we spotted a little gnome of a guy watching from a doorway down the block. Each time the sting went down, he would move a little closer to the site. Finally, it was getting about time to wrap it up when he walked up to the undercover officer and said, "I'll give you ten dollars for a blow job."

The officer doubled over in laughter as the mob scene unfolded on this worm. First, she was insulted at ten dollars then asked him, "Didn't you see the officers grabbing people talking to me?"

"Yeah."

"Well, what were you thinking?"

"I think you're so pretty I just couldn't help myself and hoped my ten dollars would work."

'Stupid is as stupid does." We finished the night booking him.

The stings worked better after the newspaper began publishing the names of those arrested. The administration demanded more enforcement. Several methods were employed. The court, as a condition of release for any prostitutes arrested on EVB, required they not be allowed within one mile of EVB. We also put two man cars out, focusing only on prostitution. The units would actually follow the girls as they walked, stopping when they stopped. After a few days of this, the girls were gone. Next, we made projects out of the johns who came looking for girls. We found any chicken shit reason to pull them over and wrote all the tickets we could think of. Did you know that your little license plate needed to be illuminated, sir? Sign here, press hard, three copies. The total effect—no more prostitutes on EVB. Mission accomplished. You would guess that. You would be wrong 'cause as soon as we cleared the streets, the brass would congratulate themselves with a pat on their backs and just as quickly remove the manpower used to accomplish this. They had driven down EVB a few times and the whores were gone. So it was back to business as usual. We surmised the brass running the show hadn't worked the streets, let alone EVB. Thus the streets went back to prostitutes within a few weeks.

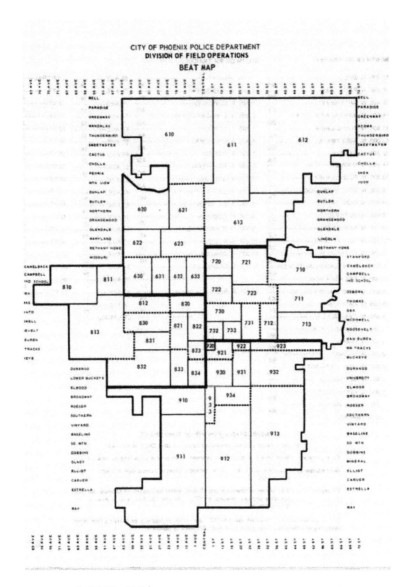

1970-80's

Note size of Beats
(yep East Van Buren)
920 921 922 923

CHAPTER 8

Random Stories from the Street, 1975 –2001

Many a shift found routine calls consuming most of your time, but in a heartbeat, it could all change. Take the case of the Circle K Bandit. Officer Jimmy W., my on-off again partner for twenty years, and I were on extensive patrol in the area of Twenty-Fourth Street and Roosevelt. We were working the late shift riding solo cars watching for miscreants, etc. Sounds good, right? actually we were goofing off in County Hospital ER's break room drinking coffee and flirting with the nurses. Our hot tone blasted the air waves: *Beeeeeeeeeeeeeeeep!* "211 in progress [armed robbery], Circle K 1600 N 24 ST." Shit, that was just around the corner. We ran out of the ER and leaped into our MOPs (mobile operating plat-forms) and raced to the scene. Holy crap, it was still in progress as we came on the scene. Jimmy pulled into the front lot while I went to the flank side, effectively cutting off any escape. The robber was just exiting the front door with a large knife held to the clerk's throat, when he noticed the police car and Jimmy pointing his .38-caliber revolver at him. Pear began discussing with this person the error of his ways. It went something like this: "Put down the knife or I'll splatter your worthless piece of shit brains all over the fucking building." Meanwhile, I had come up from Knife Man's blindside to about ten feet away. My .38 S/W was cocked with trigger pull being applied. I had assumed the Weaver shooting stance; suffice to say my gun-sights were on the side of his head. A brick wall was just behind him,

43

making for a perfect backdrop. He had no idea I was there with his full attention on Jimmy. He was about to die. In less than a second, I had run all the scenarios through my mind with this clear field of fire present. I was gonna cap him if he so much as flinched with the knife. Tunnel vision is real, and it was there that night. Picture your eye is a kaleidoscope that's slowly closing.

Sight picture was at hand as I was slowly squeezing the trigger. The side of his head looked as big as a basketball. A second lasted more like a minute as he threw down the knife, releasing the clerk. Several other police units had arrived, and he disappeared under a sea of blue uniforms. Later we learned, he had told the clerk he was gone to take him outside and kill him to prevent his being a witness. Not being able to participate in Knife Man's actual arrest, my emotions were trying to return to real time. Catching back up to the over the top feeling of having been only less than a pound of trigger pressure away from killing a person is very heavy. During all of this, I looked inside the store and saw a "customer" casually looking at the beer cases. Flashing blue lights, no less than five squad cars parked at all angles, and he was looking at the beers—*not*! Since at this moment I had no useful purpose, I went in and grabbed Mr. Innocence, who was the accomplice.

Today's police departments would hang medals and have dinners for such heroics. From our sergeant, we got a "Hurry up with your paperwork, she's holding calls." I am not lying; it was only after a downtown major read about the incident that we were recognized with a commendation letter to our files. Should have been life-saving medals. Yeah, that's what I thought.

On the street we were known as the Pear and the Bear. Jimmy the Pear for his somewhat pear-shaped body and I for—well, you can guess on that. We often rode a two-man car unlike the standard solo units. Our supervisor choose this option because we were such a dynamic duo or he had less to worry about when we were together … go figure.

Wrong Place, Wrong Time

Hot tone … I will spare the *beeeep*. "Unknown trouble." Small Chinese market on Broadway Road, around Twelfth Street. We were close and roared up to the location to find a single car parked out front. Huh … Inside was a different story. Mass hysteria would best describe it. Little Chinese guy running around with a meat cleaver screaming in broken English/Chinese and a nicely dressed black lady slumped to one side of the counter. Blood was everywhere, and another black female was trying to calm the little owner. "Get out, get out … you leave, no come back. Get out, get out!" Somebody stuff a rag in him. On closer examination, the nicely dressed lady was covered in blood all down her side that faced away from me. Wow, this was in the days before Emergency Medical Technician Service and Fire Rescue. We called for an ambulance as I ran to the squad car to retrieve my tackle box that served as our first aid kit. Me to the rescue … yeah, right. Holy shit, this gal's eyeball was hanging down her cheek by the optic nerve while the side of her face was full of shotgun pellets. She tried to raise her right hand to show me two fingers missing and third shredded. It appeared she had taken a full blast from a shotgun face on. I found a small paper cup, filled it with water, put her eyeball in it, and taped it to her face. We wrapped up her bloody wounds with gauss and waited for the ambulance. During all this, we were able to put out a description of the suspect and his vehicle. Responding units spotted and arrested the suspect, who was the unwounded female's boyfriend. The injured lady had come over to help get her sis out of her abusive relationship. With Nice Lady driving, they were westbound on Broadway Road, about Twenty-Fourth Street, when her sis noticed her asshole boyfriend following. Nice Lady, being law-abiding, stopped for the red traffic light when AH pulled alongside. Sis yelled "Duck!" and Nice Lady turned in that direction to receive a full load of no. 7 birdshot to the face and hand. The shooter took off and the girls somehow made it to the market. The ambulance arrived to transport our victim to the hospital. Detectives took it from there, and we, completing our reports, went back to the streets for more excitement.

Follow up—months later, we went to court for the aggravated assault charges. You say, why not attempted murder? Ahhhh, that would only apply to the sister he was trying to kill, not Nice Lady. Yep, you are getting ahead of me ... There they were, Sis and Asshole, arm in arm at the trial. Attempted murder charges involving Sis had been dropped for lack of her giving a shit. But he was convicted of the aggravated assault and sent away for many years. Nice Lady did lose sight in the eye I tried to save with my Dr. Kildare skill.

Always a Bears Fan ... Da Bears

It was a January Sunday in 1986 (I know because the NFL Chicago Bears in their march to Super Bowl XX were playing in a semifinal football game). It was hoped they would go to Super Bowl and win it all. Now I am and will always be a fan of Da Bears. "Bravo 913 check welfare of the elderly male" at such-and-such street. Arriving, we contacted a Meals on Wheels fellow who had called. He couldn't get a response at the apartment door for his delivery and didn't know what to do. He did know the gentlemen was old and couldn't have gone anywhere. Not a good sign, but the landlord was en route with a key, so we waited a brief time. The key arrived, allowing us entry. Inside, we found the old fellow on the floor wedged between the wall and bed. Small place—two rooms and no place to actually turn around. Jimmy checked for a pulse, announcing, "He's dead." We advised radio and our supervisor of such. No foul play suspected, Pear began checking for medication that might yield a doctor's name to be contacted. If he would sign the death certificate, this would eliminate the need for a detective to investigate. Simple enough—done it hundreds of times.

There being nothing for me to do but wait, I turned on his little black-and-white TV and tuned into the game. The place was so small I had to stand over the top of him to view the game. I was really into the game when "Ahhhhhh ahhhhhhhh" came from the little old bundle underneath me. Scared the shit out of me, but not losing a moment, I said, "*Bud!* Thought you said this guy was dead."

"He is!" was the reply.

"Well, you better come over here and tell him." We immediately came 10-8 (in service) and started scrambling.

"Roll fire rescue," we told radio. "And cancel the mortuary service." A quiet moment ensued, with me looking at Jimmy with a look of "What the f—!" Sergeant Larry O. cruised by with a very puzzled look on his face. I looked directly at him as I knew he wanted an answer and said "Lazarus" (remembering Jesus's cousin who came back to life). Sarge drove away, not saying a word. Fire arrived and took over transporting the old guy to the hospital, where he died for real a few days later.

Oh, Chicago won the game and went on to win the Super Bowl. Go, Bears!

Call it a 963?

Hot tone … Serious injury accident, Fortieth Street, south end of Sky Harbor Airport. "920 Adam handle the call." Sounded bad, but these weren't unusual calls on a weekend night.

"920A, 23 …" He had arrived at the scene.

Moments later, "920A advise 92 (sergeant), I have a 963 roll hit and run [detail that handled fatalities]." Now I just told you that we don't do that, so I had to go see what was happening. As a general condition, we were instructed not to broadcast on radio that persons were dead at the scene of car wrecks. (962 injury accident 963 fatal.) Downtown brass had sent this pearl of wisdom to the troops for some unknown reason. Maybe they had heard of Jimmy's role acting as the coroner (previous story). At the scene, emergency vehicles were parked everywhere: fire rescue, fire trucks, ambulances, and the wrecked car. Flashing lights strobing the night, right out of a Hollywood movie set … A group of firefighters came walking back out of a dark desert area. A stumbling white male was walking with them. Now I didn't get confused often, but this was one of them times.

"Chuck (920A), what the hell is going on, and how did you call a 963? We don't do that, remember?"

Chuck, a very cool, collected, and calm officer had a dazed look on his face and said, "Really ... well, take a look in the fucking car." I walked a few feet over to the somewhat torn-up car that was covered with gravel, dirt, and rocks and looked inside. Holy shit—the passenger was impaled through the top of his head with the steel fence pole. It came out just above his rectum. Shish-kebabed. Oh my god! The driver, southbound on Fortieth Street, had lost control of his car on the curves and slammed into the fence. The steel pole that runs along the top of a chained linked fence had come loose, smashing through the hood and windshield right into his passenger's head. 920 Adam was right with his 963 call; there could be no doubt this poor guy was graveyard dead.

Follow up—the 901H (dead person) was a dear long-lost high school friend of the driver. Just that day, they had hooked back up. They had grown up together back east, and today was their reunion. Following the wreck and discovery of his friend's demise, the driver had run off into the desert. It was him the firemen had brought back. He was transported to the hospital, where I had to subdue him because he didn't want to submit to alcohol or any other testing. I had to grab him by his hair with both hands and restrain him for about two minutes. He calmed down and caused no further problems while submitting to our tests. His alcohol level was 0.00. No drugs or signs of reckless driving, speed, or any wrongdoing were found, so a citation for 28-701A, "Failure to control speed to avoid a collision," was issued and he was released. We offered to transport him anywhere; he refused. I really felt helpless as I knew this was huge and couldn't begin to understand what he was feeling. An hour after his release, we got a call from the dead guy's family. The driver had called them apologizing and said he was going out to the desert to kill himself. A large search for him turned up—nothing. PS: he did turn up at the family's house the next day.

Drunks

Drunks—oh, how they are the source of most calls for service. I don't recall ever going to a violence-based call that at least one person involved hadn't been drinking. Often wondered if the stupidity level wasn't proportional to alcohol level. Usual call—family fight, see the woman ... arrive finding house a mess, usually something broken. She's crying, maybe mascara smeared. No bruises or obvious injuries. That scene is repeated hundreds of times every day in the USA. There really isn't a solution for them as most don't dislike this life enough to change it. Standard attempt to separate or get councelor help falls on deaf ears. Yada ... all suggestions rejected. Goodbye, see ya all next Friday night. Sound boring? Well, there were ways to spice it up. Changing the above scenario a little, we responded to a family fight involving two old bachelor brothers. Been there several times. Very cranky duo. Never interested in any solution. Usually neighbors had called about the noise. Officer Ray R. and I arrived to listen to their pitiful excuses for their arguing. Today's rant was, one hadn't done the dishes while the other didn't vacuum. Ray looked at me with his twinkling eyes and said, "Which chore do you want?" I chose the dishes while he turned on the vac. The brothers were speechless. In less than five minutes, we had 'er done and bid our cranky pair goodbye. I don't recall a return call.

Officers forget the public will take you at your word literally.

Pear was taking a burglary report one morning while listening to the homeowner lament about crime and criminals in general. The area involved was his small detached garage which had repeatedly been broken into.

My partner, mostly to himself, said, "If it were my property, I'd sit on the roof and shoot those sum bitches." Next shift out, we were briefed there had been a shooting involving two nighttime burglars. Could it be? It was. Whether or not our victim had taken Jimmy's advice will never be known but the story goes he made a little sniper's nest and waited. The two figures prying on his garage door's lock were greeted by no. 8 bird shot. The call from the hospital about pellet removal was the police's first knowledge of the incident.

Investigating officers were met with silence from all parties. We only knew the location as a cabbie had complained about the bloody mess they left in his taxi.

Not to be outdone ...

One of our Circle K's owners near the Barrio had complained to me about all the beer runs he was having. Typically 3-4 gang bangers come in the story, grab 2-24 packs each, split up, and run to the get-away car. "We can't chase them leaving the store open."

"We know when they come in what they're up to, but what can I do?"

I suggested if he knew who was going to steal beer lock the front door when they were inside and refused to allow them out without paying.

That solution should have gotten me an "Atta boy." The following Sunday morning, after briefing, I cruised up toward the store. From half a block away, several construction trucks in the parking lot could be seen. Slowly passing, I noticed the whole front of the store had been torn off and was lying in the parking lot. Later, I learned my advice had been taken. The perps, now safely locked inside with their attempted stolen goods, became frustrated, signaling their get-away driver to ram the doors. Ouch. He began crashing the doors in their stolen vehicle. Well, my plan looked good on paper, so they say.

An awake shift 3 officer noticed a car with pieces of aluminum and glass hanging from it driving around. The rest is history.

Working the Holidays

'Twas the Night Before Christmas (1977)

Sargent Steve S., a 6-foot, 225-pound Arizona State Powerlifting Champion, crashed through the briefing room's door, chomping on a cigar. A little wisp of smoke trailed him as he walked past the "No Smoking" sign, sliding effortlessly into his chair at the head of the room. Staring back were his troops, nine of them. They were, though they didn't know it, handpicked by him. The unwritten rule for his 92 Bravo Squad: be a sharp, smart, aggressive troop or work for someone else. No Mamzie Pampzies on his squad. Sergeant, kind of a legend and always unpredictable, truly loved his squads and troopers. 92 Bravo always lead the district's recap in arrests, calls for service, and complaints.

Police briefings were being held through the nation before squads hit the street and their assigned beats. The purpose was to advise them on items of interest. Unusual activity, special watches, etc. The moment was interrupted when Sergeant Wayne C, an alleged bad-ass, walked into the room to complain about some members of 92B Squad poaching arrests in his projects. The projects were a special area of the city to be patrolled only by "his" squad. He tried to berate us and went on ranting as Sergeant Steve S. slowly stopped reading our briefing and approached Wayne. Steve put him in a bear hug, lifting him off his feet and threw him through the door. The door collapsed as Sergeant Wayne C. crashed into the opposite wall, which broke apart. It was a site to behold.

As the dust and plaster settled, Sergeant Steve said, "Wayne, how many times have I told you, don't come in my briefings unless you bring some beef for my meat eaters?" We were stunned. Sergeant C. collected himself as best he could and walked away, muttering something about "crazy MF."

Sgt. Wayne interrupting our briefing was, it being Christmas Eve, Sgt. Steve's annual reading of "Twas the Night before Christmas" was being delayed. Sergeant propped the door back up, returned to his seat, and reverently began, "'Twas the night before Christmas and all through ..."

Another Christmas Eve. The night had turned gloomy with a dampness in the air driving our already dampened spirts down further. Working holidays always was a bummer. Older officers would volunteer for the duty, so younger cops with kids could be off. Still, there was time to reflect on family and the season. The seemingly serine moment was broken when radio advised the traffic lights were out at Twentieth Street and Washington. Located at that spot was a Mexican club, El Calderon, known for its rowdy drinking and general hell-raising. Ricky R. (reputed to be a direct descendant of the infamous outlaw) Johnny Ringo had gotten the call. I, knowing his lack of fondness for our brown-skinned south-of-the-border brothers, joined him on the call. The rain was just slightly falling as I pulled up. The lights were indeed out (probably from someone stripping the wire for its copper somewhere).

We set some flares and gave the stink-eye to patrons from the bar who had begun gathering.

Maybe a little background on the El Calderon would help clarify. Certain areas in Phoenix had always been known to cater to different ethnic groups. El Calderon was the Mexicans' place, thus they tried to display an attitude of "It's ours, stay away." Wrong, we were charged with keeping a lid on and maintaining a police presence throughout the district. We went anywhere at anytime, and to interfere with us meant a trip to jail if not the hospital. Not braggadocios, just the way it was. On occasion, the club's patrons could become a little bit argumentative when we need to make an arrest. This would result in a very concentrated effort of special action to their activities. What I am really saying is we kicked any and all asses around there for a week or so until if we arrive for a problem, the gents would hold the door open, pointing out the problem parties. Blacks, whites, Mexicans—all people understood who's in charge.

Back to Christmas Eve and the traffic lights. Ricky and I were standing in the street light by the flares as the traffic was passing by when Sergeant Steve S. pulled up, parked, and approached us.

He looked at the twenty or so Mexicans gathered and told us, "We are going to sing Christmas carols and the crowd will be our chorus."

Really! We started off with "We Three Kings," a rousing rendition it was. Sgt. Steve talked to the gathered group, and soon we were all singing the favorites. Now mind you, they were singing in Spanish and could have been saying "Kill the pigs" for all we knew, but they were staying with the rhythm. That event probably did more for race relations than all the community development bullshit.

Holidays are a time for family gatherings. In the Mexican families, during the holidays, there seemed to be a supreme effort to gather the clan for dinners to please Nana. Noble thought, but in practice not so good. Maybe it was isolated to the barrows I worked in, but you could almost set your watch to about 1:00 p.m. for the family fights to begin. Prior to the Sky Harbor Airport expansion, consider the whole family, including several generations—all lived within walking distance of each other. It wouldn't seem that gathering should have any problem. Oh, but it did. Uncles, aunts, brothers, cousins all were in the room, remembering why they hadn't spoken for over a year.

Probably last year's gathering had resulted in a huge fight with several being hauled off to jail, hospital, or both. First it would be accusations then outright lies. The availability of carving knives only added to the mayhem to come. Angry words turned into action with some of the more sober calling the police.

Poor Nana would cry, and Grandpa would say "No mas." Several times at the county hospital I heard doctors talking about the serious infections that turkey and trimming would cause on the stab wounds brought in.

Patrolling this same area on a holiday I spotted an old beat-up junker exiting the El Calderon's parking lot. It had caught my eye as its headlights weren't turned on. It proceeded west down Washington Street lightless. I caught up to it after a few blocks. I lit it up and, it pulled to the curb immediately. Good sign, most likely not a DUI. I contacted the driver, a Mexican about twenty-five years old. Through the driver and his five passengers' broken English, I learned he was the designated driver. Great, he was sober … except he didn't have a driver's license. The car had no registration, insurance, or valid paperwork. I had everyone exit the car and discovered nary a driver license or ID among them.

What was the chance that deep in Phoenix's Mexican barrio I would stop a car with six people who spoke no English and had no IDs? Actually, pretty good. I gathered enough information on the driver and wrote him a six-pack of tickets. I warned through my broken Spanish the car was not to be driven and left the little gaggle standing on the sidewalk. I went about answering calls, and about an hour later, what do I see cruising along, this time with its light on? Yep, you guessed it—my six banditos. Assuming he hadn't made a trip to MVD since our last encounter, I pulled him over again and wrote out another six-pack. Thankfully, that was the last I saw of them, I thought.

A week or so later, I was summoned to the captain's office to explain why I had written twelve tickets to a poor, hapless Mexican.

My sergeant, who knew the story, told me to hit the street, and he would explain to our poor excuse for a captain the facts of street life. Case closed.

The Arm

Once in a while, a "Put this in indelible ink" event occurs.

It all began on a normal night, if such existed on EVB. Radio cleared me to go to the county hospital's Physic Unit. Unknown issue but no need to rush. That piqued my interest since I didn't like going there anyway. A visit required removal of your sidearm, which made you feel naked. The Pear, hearing the call, double-clicked his mic, code for "I'm following in." Supervisors didn't like two cars going to a seemingly one-car call. They had their rules, and we had ours. I was being sent to a facility full of whacked-out "can't function in society" people, so what could possibly go wrong? Duh!

The building, offset from the main hospital, is a small complex requiring a series of locked doors to enter. *Buzz.*

"Yes."

"Police."

"Yes."

"Um, you called me."

"Oh, just a minute."

Who the hell did they think was staring at their camera in my nicely pressed uniform and shined boots, Bozo the Clown? Several minutes passed while I considered my escape but heard the door's buzzer sound. Crap, no way out now. At the next door, same routine. *Buzzzz.*

"Yes."

"Just open the door, nitwit."

Came out before I could catch it. Inside the door, buzzer was miffed I hadn't found his humor side splitting. "Can you find the person who called for the police please?" A gnome-looking inmate went off in search of the caller. I amused myself watching the Pear play the twit's buzz-buzz game. Jimmy wasn't near as pleasant as me when he was allowed inside. His mother would have used a bar of soap on his mouth.

Female doctor came out to greet us with a big smile, saying she were sorry to bother us, but a very unusual situation had occurred and she didn't know where else to turn.

"What?"

"Well, let me tell you and show you at the same time."

This was becoming an Ellery Queen Mystery. We followed her through another buzzed door to find ourselves in a lab-type room. On the table was a big bucket covered by a towel. She removed the towel, and there in the bucket in full view was an arm, hand and shoulder complete. The air was sucked out of the room as we both took in the moment.

Doctor said, "Yep, that was my reaction too."

"What the hell?" was my first comment.

"Please let me explain."

Earlier this evening, a phone call had come in from an unidentified male. He want to know what he could do with an arm and shoulder his roommate was eating. The doctor played the following recording for us.

"Who does the limb belong to?"

"Oh, it's his—it was cut off in an industrial accident years ago."

She went on, "Well, what's the problem today?"

"He keeps it frozen, and he has begun slicing off pieces and frying it with his eggs for breakfast."

Stalling for time, she said, "Well, that does seem to be an issue." Playing the game, she asked, "What did he keep it for?"

"Oh, he liked to put money in the fingers and hand it to tellers at drive-throughs. Scared people that way."

She was still thinking this was a hoax (pronounced *hoe-axe* in the South); she suggested he bring it by the facility for disposal. He agreed and, without asking for their location, hung up. That settled it—just another loon in a long parade of um.

Near an hour later, there was a buzz on the twit's door, but no one was there. Strange but a further look found a towel-wrapped object on the entrance step. Oh yeah, the aforementioned appendage was now lying in a bucket covered with ice. Their dilemma began and ended by icing it and calling us. What the hell was I to do with a frozen human hand, arm, and shoulder?

Ah, but first things first. It was off to Coco's diner for suppertime and a place to make calls, hoping to find a home for our frozen bundle. While waiting for my dinner, I located a representative from the County Morgue, who agreed to take possession of the limb. Our waitress, a feisty thing, always wanted in on the latest excitement from the street. The arm caper should work, we thought. She outright called us liars when the story was revealed. A trip out to the trunk of my car had her screaming. "OMG! OMG! OMG!" she repeated over and over again. It took a while to rein her in and get back to work.

I transported the appendage to the morgue, who told me state law in Wyoming allowed a person to keep body parts removed from them.

A couple nights later, I dropped in for dinner at Coco's, and our girl was working. She had blown off the incident and took my order. "No," she said, "you need fries with that."

Whatever. My meal came out with the two other waitresses following her. The fries were in a little, boat which upon closer view had a little plastic hand and arm in among them. Yep, Barbie had given up her arm for this joke.

Shoot a Wall

Often folks will ask, "Did you ever shoot anyone?" Never was sure why they thought they needed to know. The answer, well ... I did shoot something while on duty.

Working 900 District and driving the sergeant, I was sitting watching my supervisor fill out seemingly reams of paperwork. Reminded me why I didn't want to follow the promotional route. District radio dispatch info was being broadest throughout the building. The routine chatter was broken by a very stressed 906 call at 2500 East Van Buren The Airporter ... hotel. I'll explain: 907 (need a backup), 906 (need help right now!), 998 (officer involved in shooting), 999 (most extreme call for help).

Add the amount of stress in the officer's voice and multiply each of the above accordingly. We were out the door and Code 3 to the location. A lot of activity met us. One officer with blood on his hands was being put on a stretcher near an ambulance. Small groups of two to three officers were huddling while a crowd was milling around. Boss asked for details on the incident. Vague would best describe the answers. Something about officer shot; suspects ran into room 109. A posse was formed and headed for the room, short only of their noose. Guns drawn the door for 109 was pushed open. Sergeant led the officers into the room. Just then, I saw a blur to my right run past me, saying, "I'll take care of this shit." Not so fast, Buckwheat. I grabbed his neck and launched him into the wall. He came back off the wall, trying to escape only to be slammed back again. A very loud *boom* shook the scene. The yelling of "Hands up, freeze!" etc. from inside the room, stopped. I looked down at my still-smoking .38-cal S/W revolver in my right hand. Holy crap, I had just fired a round. Sergeant stuck his head out of the room and said, "Who'd we shoot, Fribbo?"

"No one, an accident" was all I could mutter.

Another officer took my now very still and quiet offender away with nary a struggle. A one-and-a-half-inch long gouge mark on the wall stared back at me. Nice little pile of cement dust lay right below.

One officer was checking his pants cuffs but found only some cement debris. The blast must have rattled his pant. My little scene, having injured no one, became insignificant. The takedown had occurred also with no one hurt, so we were wrapping up just another incident on EVB. Turned out the original call was johns fighting with hookers. Who knew or really cared why? Arriving units, probably looking for recap arrests, tried to separate the warring factions. Bad idea since the johns, realizing a trip to jail wouldn't be the best conversation around Sunday's dinner table, wanted to make a hasty exit. Prostitutes, their friends, and the general public all turned on the police, trying to rescue the hapless johns. Flashlights, being a handy tool for officers, began to appear. One problem with our issued Ray-O-Vacs, both ends tended to fly off when used as a club. Our scene was littered with batteries, lenses, and end caps. The officer with blood on him leaving with the ambulance had the suspects type "O" blood on him. Seemed during the attempted arrest of that one participant, whose head had help dismantle a flashlight, the blood had been exchanged. Following that, the same officer had been knocked on his butt, thus the trip to the hospital.

A calm was returning as some units tried to sort out the particulars. Sergeant announced I would return to the station with him. There I would give him my gun and complete my AD (accidental discharge) report. Almost sounds dirty, huh?

My shooting was declared legit and blamed on a thing called sympathetic response. When my left hand grabbed my fellow's neck and squeezed, so did my right hand with a finger on the trigger. *Boom* was the result. I recall at least two deaths resulting from this problem. I think the "Keep your finger off the trigger till you're ready to shoot" memo came out around then. Some years later (bless their hearts), an outfit developed an aluminum-tube flashlight. Almost looked like a night stick with ten to twelve batteries in it.

Lost Cat/Found Cat

Once or twice in every officer's career comes a moment so different it becomes legendary. My event.

Patrolling EVB on a warm summer night got a call to see the lady "no tell motel' reference criminal damage to her property.

How could anyone do damage to the area since total value of the place wasn't a dollar two eighty? "Just get over there, Officer and do your job," my little conscience spoke. I pulled into the twelve-unit 1940s-cabin-style lodging. A frustrated and disheveled innkeeper met us. Pear was bored so he followed in on the call. The large rollers and flowing bathrobe indicated an "early to bed or I never remove them" appearance.

"How may your Phoenix police assist?" Yep, I was very formal that night.

"Those damn kids wrecked the room. I rented them and ran off without paying for the second night."

"Oh yeah, and they stole my cat, Tabby."

"How do you know they stole your cat?" I foolishly asked.

"Do you see him around?" That part of the investigation settled, she led us to the scene of the crime. The room had been tossed, along with several pieces of furniture broken. Strangely, the front panel of the dresser drawer was lying on the floor, the dovetail joints clearly visible. Never seen that before. Our innkeeper was bitching so much about this younger generation I asked her to go to her office and await our arrival. At first, it was a slight hissing sound. Where was it coming from? Was it the elusive Tabby? What the hell were we hearing? The movement at the bottom of the curtain gave us a hint. I slowly pulled it back to reveal a huge python snake. Holy crap—it was curled up, looking about one hundred feet long. I advised radio of the find, knowing every squad member would have to come see this. The snake wasn't aggressive, actually content. While an interesting situation, what should we do about it? On cue, the units began to arrive with all kinds of suggestions. I'll name a few: "Take it downtown and leave in the Chief's office." "Start our own sideshow." "Make it your backup." You get the idea.

Snake Left in a Motel Room
On East Van Buren St (EVB)

Animal control advised they would take custody if we could get it to them. Figuring out who owned it was secondary to securing it tonight. A patty wagon was ordered with a fifty-five-gallon barrel. A burlap sack completed the capture kit. Six of our larger officers prepared to wrestle our now named "Congo" snake out to the wagon for transport.

On a count, we each grabbed a piece, stretching it out. It proved to be about sixteen feet long and ten inches around except midway down its girth, which expanded to sixteen to eighteen inches around. The search for Tabby was canceled. We waited near the street for the wagon's arrival, amusing ourselves by letting Congo try to coil, then we would straighten her back out. It was quite a workout. The double takes of the passing drivers was priceless. Congo snug in her new barrel home, I went to finish my report on the criminal damage. The office was dark, which hinted she had forgotten or didn't care anymore. 10-8 (back in service).

Congo had been part of a burglary committed by some teens on the west side of the city. She, along with many reptiles, were stolen. All the critters were recovered and returned to their homes.

On a quiet Sunday morning … not always

I was on routine patrol cruising as dawn was breaking on another Sunday. The effects of Saturday night evident with the usual array of illegally parked cars and trash littering the streets. Usually, the creatures were worn out by dawn, and a period of quiet followed. A newer model foreign car passed me (since 1955, I couldn't tell one car from another) eastbound on McDowell Road around 7 ST. Male driver, twenties, avoided looking at me and had four brand new tires in the back seat. They still had the nubbins on them. You say, "Wow, that's some observation for a quick glance"? That's what you paid me the big bucks for. I U-turned, pulled in behind it, and found some chicken shit violation to stop it and lit him up. Coasting to the curb, he never looked back at me. All signs that weren't normal thus suspicious. I walked up to the driver. "Need your driver's license, registration, and proof of insurance …" How many times have I said that in my career? He didn't have any of the three—bingo!

"Who does the car belong to?"

"Huh, a guy."

"Does he have a name?"

"Larry I think."

"I see, does he know you have the car?"

"Huh, yeah, I think." You are getting the picture—mostly the stupid ones get caught. NCIC (National Crime Information Center) check was running as I was unraveling his story. The car came back, no wants or warrants for it and the name he gave me. Keys were in the car, but often stolen cars overnight haven't been reported yet. How 'bout the tires that were still lined up along with a now visible floor jack?

"I bought them from a guy."

"Where and when?"

"Huh, I don't remember."

From the moment I saw him driving, I knew crime was a foot, but a little interrogation can lead to unknown places. I had heard enough when he said "a guy" to know we would be a while sorting this out. An on-duty detective monitoring my contacts with radio asked if I wanted any help. Really volunteering to assist, a first. You bet I would welcome his expertise. The detective soon arrived and faster than you could say "Jack Robinson" (very old saying). This whole deal was going downtown to police headquarters for some detailed investigation. Actually why sit out in the hot sun when an air-conditioned building awaited us. We loaded the tires, jack, and vehicle registration along with our dip-shit into my unit. I locked up "Larry's Car" and off to 620 W Washington (police headquarters) we went. D-S (first word is Dip), I will call him, was very vague and noncommittal to our questions. He didn't how to contact Larry but could find him at Metro Center. The registered owner was from Los Angeles, but no phone or address for him was found in the car. We found an invoice with a car dealer's name on some service work. The listed owner was anything but a Larry. D-S continued to be unconcerned about the dark hole he was traveling down. Very puzzling indeed. It was close to noon, and the detective called the dealership in California to try and shed any light on contacting the real owner. Picture the scene—we were in an interrogation room sitting with D-S, whom we had given a Coke. Detective slips out to the hall but in sight of us to make the call. He suddenly turned a shade of gray, set the phone on a desk, and flew into the room, grabbing D-S. This took me by surprise, but I helped him even though D-S had not resisted in any way. Secured now with handcuffs and fastened to the D ring on the table, my detective motioned for me to leave the room with him. Outside the room, I was advised the guy was possibly a murderer. *What!* What gives … NCIC had nothing on him or the car an hour ago. Now for the rest of the story:

The detective had contacted the dealership through the paperwork we found. He asked how we could get a hold of the guy whose name we had found and did he own such and such a car. Yes, he did once own that car, and no, we couldn't contact him since he was murdered a week ago. Holy crap. We contacted LAPD where the offense had occurred, who filled us in on what they knew. They requested us to see if D-S wanted to talk and go ahead with his interrogation. We read D-S his Miranda rights and asked if he wanted to talk about it.

NUMERICAL ORDER

1 Acknowledge Message
2 Urgent — No Red Light or Siren
3 Emergency — Use Red Light & Siren
4 No Further Assistance Needed
5 Stake Out—Other Units Stay Away
6 Out for Investigation (Citation, 10-20 Investigation, or etc.)
7 Out of service to Eat
101 Woman in the Car
102 Woman out of the Car
103 Subject to Call at Ext. ___
105 Going for Gas
106 Car Wash
210 Strong Armed Robbery
211 Armed Robbery
211A Armed Robbery Alarm
211B Extortion
236 Threat
237G Glue Sniffing
237U Marijuana (large amt.)
237M Report of Marijuana
237K Marijuana (small amt.)
237D Dangerous Drugs
237N Narcotics
239 Fight
240 Assault
245 Assault with a Deadly Weapon
246 Unconfirmed Report of a Sniper
246C Confirmed Report of a Sniper
261 Rape
261B Bigamy, Adultery, etc.
300 Gambling
310 Molesting
311 Indecent Exposure
312 Child Neglect (C.D.M.)
312A Child Abuse
315 Forgery
316 Bogus Check
317 Soliciting
318 Defrauding Innkeeper
319 Lost Report
390 Drunk (Disturbing, Down, In Car)
390A LARC
390C Drunk Driver
390L Liquor Violation
415A Phone Calls
415B Criminal Damage

415E Loud Music or Noise Disturbing
415F Family Row Disturbing
415G Shots Fired
415H Animals Disturbing, Barking Dog
415I Incorrigible Juvenile
415J Juveniles Disturbing
417 Subject Threatening
417B Barricade
417G Subject with a Gun
417K Subject with a Knife
418 Civil Matter-Stand By
418A Landlord — Tenant Dispute
418B Neighbor Dispute
418D Illegal Dumping
418G Unwanted Guests
418T Trespassing
451 Homicide
459 Burglary
459A Burglar Alarm (Audible/Silent)
459P Burglary From Vehicle
487 Theft
487A Theft from Person-Purse Snatch
487B Shoplifting
487F Theft from Vehicle
487I Stolen Bicycle
487L Locate Only, Vehicle
487P Police Car Stolen
487V Stolen Vehicle
488I Recovered Bicycle
488L Recovery of Locate Only, Vehicle
488V Recovery of Vehicle
491 Kidnapping
491A Custodial Interference
508 Traffic Control (Special Detail)
515 Speeding or Racing
585 Traffic Hazard
586 Illegal Parking
601 Missing Person
601J Missing Juvenile
601F Found Missing Person
647 Suspicious Person, Check Activity
647V Suspicious Person in Vehicle, Check Activity
651 Loose Animals
651A Injured Animals
707 Bomb Scare
711 Intensive Patrol (Preventative)
900 Check Welfare
901 Injured or Sick Person
901C Cutting
901B

901G Shooting
901H Dead Body
901K Ambulance (Enroute, At Scene, or Needed)
901o Overdose Victim
912 Enroute to Hospital
914 Fire Follow-up
915 Arson
915H Hazardous Material
915B Fire Bomb
906 Officer Needs Assistance, Potentially Hazardous Situation
907 Back-Up (Make the ___ or Request for)
917 Abandoned Vehicle
918 Insane Person
921 Prowler
921P Peeping Tom
926 Wrecker from List
927 Investigate Unknown Trouble
928 Found Property
928E Found Explosives
928I Found Bicycle
928N Found Narcotics
960 Police Aircraft Down, No Injury or Property Damage
960A Police Aircraft Down, with Injury and/or Property Damage
961 Accident — No Injuries
961H Hit & Run — No Injuries
962 Accident — Injuries
962H Hit & Run — Injuries
963 Accident — Fatality
963H Hit & Run — Fatality
965 Chemist Needed (or B.A. Operator needed)
966 ID Officer Needed
968 Officer Involved in Shooting
999 Officer Needs Help Urgently

NOTE: S: Utilize the symbol "S" when a supplemental report is completed.
X: Utilize the symbol "X" when an attempted report is completed.

TEN SERIES

10 —
1 Signal Weak
2 Signal Good
3 Stop Transmitting
4 Affirmative (OK)
5 Relay (to)
6 Busy
7 Going off duty/out of service
8 In Service
9 Say again
10 Negative
11 ___ on duty
12 Stand by (stop)
13 Existing conditions (road or weather)
14 Message information
15 Message delivered
16 Reply to message
17 Enroute
18 Urgent/complete present assignment as soon as possible
19 (In) contact
20 Location
21 Call by phone
22 Disregard/take no further action
23 Arrived at scene
24 Assignment completed
25 Report to (meet)
26 Estimated arrival time
27 Driver's License/permit information
28 Ownership information/check full registration
29 Records check/warrant information
30 Danger/caution

31 Pick up papers
32 Units needed (specify)
33 Help me quick
34 Correct time
35 Reserved ___
36 Reserved ___
37 Reserved ___
38 Reserved ___
39 Reserved ___
40 Out of service — subject to call
41 Convoy or escort — mail, parade, etc.
42 Prisoner in custody or booking
43 No traffic your unit
44 Does not conform with rules and regulations
45 Emergency traffic at station
46 Checking for traffic
47 Prepare to copy
48 Officer at home
49 Confidential Information
50 Switching to ___ frequency
No. 1 Chase
2 Information
3 Detective
4 400 PRECINCT
5 500 PRECINCT
6 600 PRECINCT
7 700 PRECINCT
8 800 PRECINCT
9 900 PRECINCT
51 Felony warrant outstanding
52 Misdemeanor warrant outstanding
53 Attempt to locate — do not molest
54 Have car stopped — may be dangerous

56 Special information desired on your subject
57 You have possible dangerous subject back-up enroute
60 Female Officer needed to search female suspect
66 Clear for cancellation
68 Court attendance (court date or subpoena)
69 Court detail (Bailiff)
70 P.R. Contact (lunch, dinner, talk)
71 Police range
73 Equipment transfer
74 Minor repair vehicle (m.m. or radio)
75 Morgue detail
76 Notify owner of vehicle recovery, unable to contact by phone
77 Notify parents of juvenile detention
78 Detention detail
79 Death messages or emergency messages
81 Clinic detail
84 Stop signs down
85 Wires down (power, phone)
86 Irrigation water on street
87 Broken water mains
88 Damaged sidewalk
89 Holes in street
90 Traffic signals out of order
91 Assist stranded motorist
92 Wagon Wanted

Paperwork

RIGHT OF WAY
- Car on Rt.-Open Intersection 28-771.A
- Yield Rt.-"T" Intersection 28-771.A
- Turning Left at Intersection 28-772
- Yield from Stop Sign 28-773.B
- Yield from Private Drive 28-774
- Yield to Emergency Vehicles 28-775.A.1
- Following Fire Truck/500 Feet 28-775.A.2

PEDESTRIANS
- Pedestrian in Crosswalk 28-792.A
- Passing Vehicle Stopped for
  Pedestrian 28-792.B
- Crossing at other than Crosswalk
  (Yield to Vehicles) 28-793.A
- Jaywalking Between Signals 28-793.C
- Walking in Street where Sidewalk
  Provided 28-796.A
- Hitchhiking on Roadway 28-796.C

SCHOOL ZONES
- Speed in Excess of 15 MPH 28-797.A
- Stop for Ped. in School Crosswalk .. 28-797.C

BICYCLES
- More than one person on a Bicycle .. 28-813.B
- Clinging to Vehicle 28-814
- Ride on Right Side 28-815.A
- To use Bicycle Path 28-815.C
- Bicycle Lamps Required 28-817.A
- Brake Required 28-817.C

STOPS AND MISCELLANEOUS VIOLATIONS
- Stop at Railroad Crossing Signal .. 28-851.A
- Driving Thru/Around Closed RR Gate 28-851.B
- Bus, Explosive and Flammable Cargo
  Stop at Railroad Crossing 28-853.A
- Stop Sign 28-855.B
- Yield Sign 28-855.C
- Stop-From Alley or Drive 28-856
- Passing Stopped School Bus 28-857.A
- Backing in Safety 28-891
- Driving with Obstructed View
  (Passenger or Load Obstruction) .. 28-893.A
- Crossing Fire Hose 28-897
- Placing Hazardous Material on
  Roadway 28-898.A
- Throwing or Dropping an Object from
  Overpass 28-898.01
- Driving Upon a Sidewalk 28-904
- Door as a Traffic Obstruction 28-905
- Change Height of Moving Vehicle
  (15MPH+) 28-906
- Overweight Vehicle 28-206
- Transporting Hazardous Materials .. 28-1033
- Permitting Unlawful Operation 28-1052
- Illegal Citation Cancellation 28-1060
- Failure to Stop for Peace Officer ... 28-1075.A
- Failure of Operator to Provide Identity 28-1075.B
- Failure of Non-Operator to Provide
  Identification 28-1075.C
- Surrender of License and Registration 28-1202
- Mandatory Insurance 28-1253.D

VEHICLE EQUIPMENT
- Child Passenger Restraint 28-907.A
- When Lighted Lamps Required 28-922
- Two Headlamps Required 28-924.A
- Height Limitations of Headlamps ... 28-924.C
- Red Taillamp Required 28-925.A
- Height Limitations of Taillamps 28-925.B
- Brake Lamps Required 28-927
- White Light in Rear 28-931.C
- Dim Lights from Front 28-942.1
- Dim Lights from Rear 28-942.A.1
- Brakes Required 28-952.A
- Trailer Brakes Required 28-952.A.3
- Horn Required 28-954.A
- Muffler Required 28-955.B
- Exhaust Smoke 28-955.B
- Mirror Required 28-956
- Windshield Wipers Required 28-957.B
- Windshield Required 28-957.01
- Rear Fender Splash Guards 28-958.01.A
- Non-combustible Gas Cap Required 28-965
- Unsafe Vehicles 28-981

MOTORCYCLES
- Rider and Passenger to Have Seat .. 28-892
- Depriving a M/C Full Use of a Lane .. 28-903.A
- Passing in Same Lane Occupied by
  Vehicle 28-903.B
- M/C Between Lanes/Adjacent Rows of
  Vehicles 28-903.C
- More than 2 Abreast in a Single Lane 28-903.D
- Brakes Required 28-952.A.2
- Muffler Required (includes Pvt. Prop.) 28-955.01.A
- Helmets and Goggles or Windshield 28-964.A
- Eye Protection 28-964.A
- Rear View Mirror, Seat, and Footrest 28-964.B
- Handlebar not to Exceed 15" 28-964.C

LOADS
- Red Flags on 4' to Rear 28-935
- Over Width of 8' 28-1002.A
- Projecting Load-Passenger Vehicle .. 28-1003
- Over Height of 13'6" 28-1004.A
- Over Length-Single Vehicle 40' 28-1004.D
- Over Length-Combination 65' 28-1004.E
- Projecting Loads-Front and Rear ... 28-1005.A
- Spilling Load on Roadway 28-1006.A
- Space Between Towed Vehicles
  (15' Max.) 28-1007.A
- Single Axle Load Limit 28-1008**
- Gross Weight of Vehicle 28-1009**
- Gross Weight (State Highways) 28-1009.01
- Weighing Vehicles 28-1010.C
                                          (& 1014)

CITY CODES
- Alley Speed Limit (15 MPH) 36-43
- U-Turns 36-47
- Obedience to Temporary Signs and
  Markers 36-54
- Blocking Intersection or Crosswalk 36-57
- Alley as Thoroughfare 36-61
- Driving on Dusty Lot 36-62
- Driving off Road in City Park 36-64.A

- Riding Outside of Vehicle 36-67
- Noisy Vehicle 36-68
- Squealing Tires 36-69
- Truck on a Non-major Street 36-86

PARKING CODES (All Are Civil)
- Stopping, Standing or Parking
  Prohibited 36-134
  (With appropriate Subsection as follows)
  (1) On a Sidewalk
  (2) Blocking Driveway or
       Alley Entrance
  (3) Within an Intersection
  (4) Prohibited by Signs or Red Curbs
  (5) Within 15' of a Fire Hydrant
  (6) On a Crosswalk
  (7) Within 20' of X-Walk at an
       Intersection
  (8) Within 30' of Flashing Beacon,
       Stop Sign or Traffic Control Signal
  (9) At a Designated Bus Stop
  (10) Within 50' of Nearest Rail at
        RR X-ing, or 8'6" of Center of
        RR Track.
        (except to load or unload RR cars)
  (11) Within 20' of Entrance to
        Fire Station and on Side of Street
        Opposite the Entrance,
        75' When Posted
  (12) Alongside or Opposite Any Street
        Excavation or Obstructions When
        Stopping, Standing, or Parking
        Would Impede Traffic
  (13) On Roadway Side of Any Vehicle
        Stopped or Parked at the Edge
        or Curb of Street
  (14) Upon Bridge or Elevated Structure
        or Within Street Tunnel
  (15) Area Between Curb and Sidewalk

- Parking so as to Impede Traffic ... 36-136
- Parking in Alley 36-137
- Parking Truck or Trailer on
  Residential St. 36-140
- Parallel Parking 36-142
- Parking in Drive or Posted Private Lot 36-144.a
- Parking for Sale on Unpaved Lots and
  Areas 36-145
- Parking on Registered and Posted
  Lots 36-148
- Disabled Parking 36-149
- Parking in Taxi Zone 36-152
- State Parking Code 28-871
                                          28-874

GEND: * Denotes civil violations.
        ** Denotes civil or criminal violations (criminal if excess weight is over 1,001 lbs. or if it is 2nd violation within 6 months).
     ***Denotes 10 day rule for arraignment, i.e., the 10th CALENDAR day, with the following exceptions:
        1. If the tenth day is a Saturday or Sunday, the offender will be arraigned on the following Monday.
        2. If the tenth day is a legal holiday, the offender will be arraigned on the next court day.
        3. All citations issued to the same violator at the same time will have the same arraignment day.

PHOENIX POLICE DEPARTMENT TRAFFIC VIOLATION CARD   PPD 87.8

(NOTE: 36-64.B is a Criminal Violation)

Codes

PPD #29   Rev. 11/87
YOU HAVE THE RIGHT TO REMAIN SILENT

ANYTHING YOU SAY CAN BE USED AGAINST YOU IN A COURT OF LAW

YOU HAVE THE RIGHT TO THE PRESENCE OF AN ATTORNEY TO ASSIST YOU PRIOR TO QUESTIONING, AND TO BE WITH YOU DURING QUESTIONING, IF YOU SO DESIRE.

IF YOU CANNOT AFFORD AN ATTORNEY YOU HAVE THE RIGHT TO HAVE AN ATTORNEY APPOINTED FOR YOU PRIOR TO QUESTIONING.

DO YOU UNDERSTAND THESE RIGHTS?

DATE   DR#   OFF INITIALS

Miranda Rights

"Yeah, sure" was his reply. The following was his story: A week ago, he had just been released from the LA County Jail for some minor charge. He stuck out his thumb and promptly caught a ride. The male driver asked if he wanted to party. Oh course he did, and off to a bar they went. A few drinks later, the guy invited him to his house for more drinking. Away they went. At the house, his new friend wanted to have some sexual fun. D-S said, "I ain't no fucking queer, but the guy had money, so what the fuck." The guy wanted D-S to choke him out while he was pleasuring himself. I have read this isn't all that unusual for defiant-behavior people. Well, D-S must have been real good at his task as the guy checked out of this world, cashing all his chips. D-S went on without missing a beat, continuing his tale. Since the guy was now dead, he didn't need his money or his car, right? "So I took 'um." He drove to Arizona, getting stopped by the Arizona Highway Patrol (DPS) en route. We had found that citation earlier, which only reinforced he wasn't wanted. He ran out of his small amount of stolen money soon and had found a jack and stole the tires to sell. Enter me …

We booked him with a hold for LAPD. The tires were returned to their owner a used car lot on the west side.

Follow up—a week or so later, the detective and I were contacted by the LA District Attorney's office for arrangements to come there for the preliminary hearing. It would be an over-and-back flight. We went, and he waved his hearing so that was that. Oh, you might be wondering why NCIC didn't show a hit on the car ... A VIN (vehicle ID number) letter had been entered incorrectly, thus no hit.

Radio ... Loud Party Disturbing

Radio advised "See the owner" such and such apartment complex.

Dime-a-dozen call, usually a one-to-two-man response. Contacted the complainant in the parking lot who told us he was the tenant. He advised he had a small party at his apartment that quickly got out of control, so he left. He didn't want trouble with the management, so he called us. No big deal here—we would go with him, evict the offending turds, and be 10-8 (back in service). He stated anyone refusing to leave could be arrested. One small issue, the "problems inside" had locked the door, and he didn't have his key. "Okay, will get you back in."

"Knock-knock. Police. Open the door."

"Fuck you ... go away" came the reply. Now we were standing there in full view of a large window by the door and wearing every piece of the uniform of the Phoenix Police Department. "Fuck you ... go away" was not the correct response. The AH (if you don't understand the letters, think of the orifice connected to the buttocks) came to the window and looked over the now-assembled four officers. He reached down between his legs and said, "How about you suck this, *pigs*?" Oh yeah, he leaped to number 10 on the AH scale. Picture four officers crashing into each other trying to get to the door first. *Keystone Kops* comes to mind. Remember the tenant had told us he wanted anyone in the apartment arrested for trespassing.

I thought the building was having a Magnitude 5 earthquake as first one then another rammed a boot to the door. Nothing. Shoulders hit it time and time again—nothing. This door wasn't budging. The super for the building had arrived but also didn't have a key; however, we were told a key was en route by the complex's owner.

Dip Shit came to the window and said, "Okay, I'll open the door for a sergeant." Our Sarge was already en route 'cause of the unusual amount of time we were taking on this call. I briefed him as we walked to the offending location. There, he showed Fat Boy (our new name for the Adam Henry) that he was indeed a Phoenix Sergeant of Police.

Fat Boy looked him up and down and said, "I want a real sergeant, a DPS sergeant, not you."

Sarge turned on his heel and said, "I'm 10-8 [leaving the scene] and out of here," which really meant he didn't want to be present for the opening of the door. In the front window, Fat Boy continued his little act, stroking himself and wiggling his butt. Like a shining light from heaven, the blessed key arrived. Oh my! This was going to be fun. First we showed Fat Boy we had the key, which meant he was going to be arrested. Ten cups of strong black coffee couldn't have sobered him up that fast as he tried to block the door. I used the key and was trampled for my effort by the officers behind me, rushing in to get at the now-pale-grey former antagonizer. There was not one spot exposed for me to take a shot at his blubbery body. He was "resisting" and being beaten soft.

"Ma! Ma!" was all I could hear from him between the moans. He was carted off as I continue to search the place for other cockroaches. Yep, there in a closet covered with dirty clothing was a drunk with small pieces of upchucked pizza on him. The distinctive odor of human waste (yes, he had shit his pants) wafted from him. This pathetic mass of quivering protoplasm was released and sent away. (No one would agree to book him ... figure that.) Blubber Butt went to jail, the tenant was happy to get back in his now-ramshackle apartment, and we went 10-8. Damn, that was a tough door.

Some doors just shouldn't be opened

Radio: "Strong odor coming from an apartment where the tenant hasn't been seen for days." Having been around a while, the smell of death was all too familiar as we pulled up to the location.

Well, duh. The area was in an old, decaying, and sparsely populated section of town. It wasn't homeless but the next step up. A local pointed at the door, which a blind man could have figured out from the smell. The knob turned—we were in luck. It wasn't locked, so Jimmy opened it about two inches but found it blocked. He announced our presence: "Phoenix Police, anybody home?" to the oppressive air I guess. Well, we had to go in, but why would the door be blocked? The door began to move ever so slightly as we pushed harder. Continuing to push it finally provided us enough room to slip inside. Yeah, the guy was and had been dead for several days. The obstacle blocking the door was his leg, which was wedged against the it. Seemed pushing the door against the leg meat cleaned it down toward the ankle that now had a pile of human flesh around it. The bone was clean, kinda reminded you of a cleaned turkey leg at Thanksgiving. This even grossed us out. The necessary calls were made, and the poor old guy was off to the Mortuary of the Month for disposition.

Things Aren't Always What They Appear

The Pear and the Bear were riding solo cars this AM shift. The unwritten rule was "Don't wander too far away" 'cause we were usually our only backups. I saw an elderly lady waving at me. She wasn't frantic, just seemed to need something. I cruised over to her to accept the request/information. Well, it seemed she thought her neighbor hadn't been seen since … Okay, I got the address, advised the Pear, and went 10-19 (en route). Radio was quiet, so we would do a thorough check. The house was part of the ongoing urban renewal north of the downtown. These home had been a very exclusive part of Phoenix in the olden days. Currently they were either being razed or redone as businesses. The still standing ones were mostly flop houses. Our house's front and rear doors were locked, so we began looking in windows. I spotted the old guy sitting on a couch. He was only partially visible from the distance. It appeared his head was moving, so I watched him for a minute, but nothing else moved. Shouting to him got no response. We found an open window and climbed in. His moving head was maggots crawling in and out his eye sockets. It was totally gross. No foul play was suspected, so it was a Mortuary of the Month time again. And the beat goes on.

CHAPTER 9

High-Speed Pursuits

Without a doubt, high speed pursuits are the ultimate thrill while working the streets. The announcement "I am in pursuit" got any and all's attention. A fresh cup of coffee would even be tossed to go be involved. Let me explain the dynamics. In the early days of my career, supervisors didn't try to control the number of cars involved, which of course dramatically increased the longer the pursuit continued. Crossing into other cities usual got their units involved. It was very exciting, and we often had 10-15 cars chasing these fools. Problem was far too often, an innocent civilian would end this incident by being crashed into. At the conclusion, if the fool hadn't been wrecked/injured, they would receive a thumping. The price they paid for endangering so many lives, known then as "street justice."

This night I had been assigned a rookie. Word was Lance G needed a lot of polishing. Young hard charger but acting a bit salty for his neophyte status. Give him to the Bear ... right. He wanted to drive—*no*! He wanted to go south of the river looking for action—*no*! *Sit down, shut up and learn!*

We were on the corner of Seventh Street and Mohave. I called this area Krylonville for the numerous empty cans of spray paint found everywhere. Also known as Point Taco. The complainant we were talking to had some convoluted long, drawn-out story about some thieves and boogeymen who had taken his property, yada yada yada ... I was letting the rookie try to figure out how to get us out of this. The Pear drove by as I gave him a four-finger signal that meant it was code 4 (everything was fine, no assistance needed). Moments later, Pear went code 6 (stopping a vehicle) a few blocks from us. Jimmy's radio transmission, "Code 6 300 East Mohave with Henry Adam, ahhhh shit, he's doing a donut, heading back east. I'm in pursuit." Our location put us in the grandstands as they came wailing right past us.

"Goodbye, sir, have a nice life." We were off to the races. Jimmy's unit raced north on Seventh Street, lights blazing and siren blaring. We pulled in right behind him while I advised the rookie to tell radio we would call the pursuit. This was standard procedure to allow the lead car to devote their full attention to driving. This incident was turning out to be a great training exercise, or so I thought.

I noticed my rookie didn't have on his seatbelt. "Get your belt *on*."

"I don't wear one."

"*Get it on now* and advise radio where we are." Saturday night meant lots of traffic as we flew North with both cars lights and sirens screaming. Estimated speed, 70 mph plus.

Radio asked, "Location of the pursuit?"

My rookie advised "North from Thomas Road," as later attested on the audio tapes. Well, he was right—the chase was now north of Thomas Road, but we weren't. A very large Lincoln was sitting facing south in the left-turn lane for eastbound traffic. The traffic light was green for north/southbound traffic. I was demonstrating the proper method to clear an intersection by flashing our spotlight back and forth across it. This was to get the driver's attention. I even changed our siren's sound to the European style of *wwwwwwah wawwww-wwah*. The rookie was getting a lot to remember. Some twenty feet south of the intersection, I saw the Lincoln seem to leap up, starting its eastbound turn. How do I know it was twenty feet? That's where my skid marks started. The impact was horrific. Screeching grinding crushing all wrapped together. I went blank for maybe a sec. All was silent before I noticed smoke coming from under the dash. A quick glance at the rookie saw him slumped forward, not moving. He had put on his seatbelt after all. The smoke being utmost on my mind I began to un-ass the wreckage. I found my door was jammed shut, so I was in the process of rolling the window down when it was yanked open. Freed, I was being led to an ambulance. Where did that come from? My first thought, *I am okay*, following this terrific crash. Not so fast, Doctor Fribbs. My sternum was flapping as I walked, and was that blood running down my face? Yep. Why was my stomach beginning to hurt so bad? I was placed in the ambulance (it had just happened on the scene) and removed my gun belt in hopes of easing the stomach pain. Wow, now I was really beginning to hurt. Rookie was loaded onboard, unconscious—not a good sign. Off we raced to the hospital. I was hurting but glad to be alive.

We arrived to a flurry of activity. Nurses, doctors, aides were all over us. I was having trouble processing this as I was the in-charge guy and was having no control over this. By now, my hips were really hurting, and I wanted something for the pain. Not going to happen. "You have too many injuries." Huh … Seems a method of evaluating your injuries is noting the location of your pain.

"Just give me a jar of morphine and go away." X-rays were ordered, which along with removing my clothing was next. "Hold the horses, bud, what are you doing with those shears? Don't cut off my well broke in spit shinned boots. "It will hurt a lot if we try to pull them off."

"Don't care—don't cut off my boots." Ever make a decision you later regretted? That was one for me. Holy crap, did I reach a new level on the pain scale but saved my boots. Off to X-rays I was whisked to learn how cold those metal tables can be. Nothing broken. My hip pain was the result of the seatbelt crushing my stomach area. We didn't have shoulder belts yet, which would have greatly reduced my problems. Things were calming down some when a doctor stuck a needle into my face right under my nose. I wasn't ready for this sting from one thousand bumble bees and advised him that he had been born of an illegal mother. Yes, "You SOB" was my response.

"Now, now, remember I am the guy fixing you up" was his reply. I had a good-sized cut under my nose he was to sew up. Could have prepared me for it, was my thought. Weeks later, it was discovered that my nose was also broken—how did he miss that? Maybe I pissed him off talking about his lineage.

No blood was found in my urine, so they were about done with me when a nurse (we will call her Angel) whispered, "You are gonna like this." A wonderful injection into my IV drip and I went dreamy. I was declared to have nothing seriously wrong (easy for them to say) and shipped up to a room for overnight observation. My medication put me in La La Land. Three hours had passed, and I was very tired. They left me alone, and I awoke an hour later needing to go pee big-time. Still hooked up to my IV, all of us began the journey to the head. I was bent nearly doubled as Angel's magic potion was wearing off. I was really hurting again. My business finished, the route back to the bed was retraced. I leaned back to get in the bed when my whole body locked up tight. Picture me slightly on the bed and bent at a forty-five-degree angle. I couldn't move. I was really screwed since the nurse had cautioned me about getting out of bed without calling for help. I couldn't reach the "Help me" button, so there I was. Seemed like an hour before a nurse came in to find me. She was most pissed 'cause I went pee in the bowl so they didn't know how much urine I had past. My bad.

Follow Up—went home the next day with my back doing spasms every couple of minutes. I could have been a poster boy for a chiropractor office. If you have been there, you know the feeling that any sec you will seize. My injuries were a broken sternum, three detached ribs, a broken nose, severely bruised stomach muscles, crushed pads on both elbows and knees, and some stitches. It seems that in spite of having a seatbelt on, I had still hit the windshield. Rookie, who had followed my advice, had torn intestines caused by the seatbelt cutting into him. Bad, however, it saved him from being launched through the windshield. All and all not too bad, considering we had T-Boned the Lincoln at seventy-plus mph (investigating officer's estimate). The Lincoln's driver showed .24 on the BA (Breathalyzer). Three times legal limit. He had no explanation for turning right in front of me—just another drunk out terrorizing the driving public. His passenger (boyfriend) was quiet seriously injured since he took most of the impact on his side of the car. Right leg was broken in three places for openers. Their story—they had been together all day bar hopping and were very drunk when they left the last bar. The collision had knocked their Lincoln seventy feet back in the direction it had come while destroying the whole front end of our cruiser a, '78 Plymouth. Oh yeah … what happened to the violator that started this whole thing?

He was a punk kid driving drunk on a suspended license. The units chased him around the city for fifteen minutes, finally cornering him over on the west side. When searched, the AH had a copy of a citation received early that evening. Checking the time when he was stopped showed he was already drunk then and never checked for a valid license. Never got an answer on that. I would be out of action for two weeks before it was discovered my nose was broken and would require surgery to repair. It was never pretty, but it was my only nose, so off I went to get 'er done. This would be an in-and-out procedure. I had to go in the night before so Knifeman would be ready to slice first thing in the morning.

Got to the hospital, checked in, and was sent to my room. No roommate, so I sat down in an easy chair and turned on the TV. A pleasant nurse came in and asked, "Who are you?"

Told her, "Why aren't you in your bed clothes?"

"Why should I, are we getting ready to go to work?"

She huffed off to return later with a female gorilla in nurse's garb. "You *will* get your bed clothes on now," she grunted out.

"Okay, okay, geeeeez, keep your panties on," was my reply. Hey, I was paying the bills here, right?

Early next morning, they bundled me up and wheeled me to the OR. A doctor put an IV in my arm, and I was soon floating among the tulips. Now surgery, ain't nothing to it when you go in. Once they juice you up, they could cut off your toes; you wouldn't care. They could have sewed a Bozo the Clown nose on me; I was out.

Coming out is a different story … My face was swollen with both eyes blackened. Felt like Reggie Jackson had hit a home run off my head. I could only breath through my mouth since my nose was filled with yards of gauze. The stuffing was to keep it straightened while healing. A mouth breather I wasn't and slept little for the next week. I was miserable and counting the days then hours till the nose stuffing was to come out. I was scheduled in for a late-afternoon removal when I told my wife to get an earlier slot as I was going crazy. She tried but said, "Sorry, they can't get you in early."

"Great, then tell the SOB [there I go again] I'm pulling this shit out right now."

"Yes, okay, I'll bring him right over." Musta heard me, huh? The relief I felt after he pulled over a yard of gauze out of each nostril cannot be explained.

Just thinking will out produce raw effort

I'll explain with an example. Working day shift downtown on a routine day with only a few calls for services.

Hot tone—*beeeeeeeeep.* "District 4 is in pursuit of a stolen vehicle, northbound, Seventh Avenue from Washington." *Yeah, boy, coming right at me.* I headed south on Seventh Avenue from Thomas Road, which would intercept this offender. I saw the suspect and pursuing units turn west on McDowell when the lead officer advises they turned north in the alley. I was right there, racing through the alley to head off this prick. He must have seen me coming 'cause he slammed on his breaks and bailed out. I was right behind him by about twenty-five feet. He saw me and ran west, climbing the block fence facing the alley. *Okay, let's slow this action down, think slooooooooww motion.* I was 6 feet, 220 lbs., and not in my best shape. So climbing and jumping fences was not happening! I tried the gate—it was unlocked—and through it, I went listening to the perp crashing across the yard. Out to the street, I was right behind him. He saw me and crossed the street to the next yard, where it was up and over another fence, still westbound. I tried the gate—yep, it was unlocked; I was still with the runner. Racing through this yard, he began to falter as he climbed the front fence and landed in a heap in the front yard. I walked over to his gasping body and place him in handcuffs as I hummed a few bars of "I Fought the Law and the Law Won."

While trying to catch his breath, he said, "How did you keep up with me? You're an old guy."

I told him, "Never underestimate the power of the law, son!" He never knew the first locked gate I came to would have been the end of my foot pursuit.

Deer Tag Incident

The following story was relayed to me by a very reliable officer/ sergeant. Central Avenue South was a very rough and lawless part of Phoenix in the late seventies to eighties. A string of armed robberies had taken place, and units were trying to pay special attention to the numerous small businesses along its length. Two sergeant's from adjoining squads were riding together and were roaming to help watch for trouble. Hot tone—*beeeeeeep*. 211 (armed robbery just occurred) fast food joint something, South Central. A brief description of the suspects and getaway car was broadcast as units converged to the location. The sergeants mentioned began roaming the area, looking for the suspect car. The gods of crime fighting were smiling down that night as the 211 suspect's car went roaring past them. The turds looked at them and flipped the sergeant's off. Over the years, it never failed to amaze me the audacity of crooks. The chase was on as the bandits began firing rounds at our two sergeant's. That will get your undivided attention. The non-driving sergeant put his hand gun on the dash after he figured he couldn't fire back in a residential neighborhood. The gun began sliding back and forth across the dash as they rounded each corner. The suspect's car suddenly turned into a driveway, stopping abruptly. The driver jumped out, running away while the passenger opened his door and took a shooting stance. The shooter was wearing a duster similar to the style Old West Cowboys had, as he fired off rounds. Sergeant, now less his hand-gun, unracked the unit's shotgun, racked a round into the chamber all in one motion. He returned three quick double aught buck shotguns rounds at the shooter, watching his duster flap like it was being blown in the wind. Each shotgun round contained nine .32-caliber bullets, so twenty-seven rounds went downrange in mere seconds. Duster man was discouraged and now ran into the backyard of the house. He didn't get more than about twenty feet where his ventilated body shut down, dropping him graveyard dead. It was all over in a couple of heartbeats. Arriving units found the driver hiding and took him into custody. This was a major incident, so all settled in for what they knew would be a long night of answering the detective and supervisor's questions. The two sergeants had turned the scene over to their officers when they heard conversations and laughter coming from the backyard. Of course this piqued their interest, so they went to look and see. Three of the officers were standing by the body where one had tied a deer tag (hunter tag issued by the state to use for marking kills during hunting season) to the dead guy's duster. A Polaroid camera had been found, and pictures were being taken similar to the photos you see of big game hunters with their downed trophy animal. Yep, there it was. This incident was deemed not to be happening, and the tag was removed. All the pictures were collected (or were they?), and personnel were ordered to forget this photo op ever happened. I was told a picture did escape to live for future generations to view.

Pursuits

Years later, police management, who wouldn't know real police work if it bit them on the ass, told us how to conduct a pursuit. Two units only behind the offender with one or two units paralleling—that was it. Severe punishment would befall offenders. In the famous words of Officer Bobby W., "just smile and nod." Of course we would now follow these orders to a tee ... somehow, at the end of the chase, there were usually ten to twelve cars just like before. The secret was you didn't advise radio you were involved.

The new squad alignment allowed for some squads to be doubled on certain nights—ours was Saturday. When that happened, we could work in unmarked cars. "I'm in pursuit" broke the airways … here we go again. A marked unit from another district was behind a vehicle wanted for traffic violations. As an unmarked unit, we had to stay out of the way but kinda trailed along as it went north then south then U-turned, heading back again. By now, I was getting fed up with this prick. The pursuit vehicle advised the chase had ended a few blocks from us, so we went to have a look. Remember, we were in a plain wrapped car but uniformed. The suspect, out of his car, surrounded by several officers was standing defiantly as we walked up, grabbed him, spun him around, and head planted him on the hood of the car.

"Give me your cuffs," I instructed the nearest uniformed offi-cer. Nicely cuffed and sporting a lump on his forehead, he was now being properly respectful of his situation as we departed, leaving the uniforms to wonder who were those masked men. Later, radio did clear a blind call for the plainclothes car working in the area … Yeah right, we're gonna answer that.

Often, when a commandment came down from on high (com-mand staff ordering a new way to do something) it was soon shown how foolish it was.

"I am in pursuit" cracked the airways again, gathering every-one's attention. The call came from the next district. Description of the offender was broadcast; however, the chase was far away. This all changed as the pursuit raced into our district and toward our area. Soon they were on our doorstep. A supervisor advised us to stay out of it as the required number of cars were already engaged. Yeah, right. Shortly after it started, it stopped. The units had lost the offender. Ten minutes later, the chase was on again, but now our district was running it. The offending car had tried to run over an officer, which now made it very personal. The crimes committed by this fool were adding up. Jimmy driving, we set off to right this transgression. Yeeee-hawwww, we caught up to the daisy chain (term for a line of cars in a chase), and away we went. Of course, no one checked on to advise radio. One unit got between us and the offender as we raced east with lights and sirens blaring. We entered Tempe, who joined in; next came Mesa, adding a couple more cars. Not to be outdone, Highway

Patrol soon joined into our now parade of units. We were leaving the urban areas, heading to the Salt River Indian Reservation, way east of our city. The offender slid sideways onto a dirt road, throwing up huge layers of dust. We backed off some while, driving blind through the cloud as we watched first the suspect then the first police car behind sail Evil Knievel–style off the dead-end road. Seemed the road had been built to this point then just ceased. The drop-off was about ten feet, and both cars appeared to explode as they hit terra firma. Jimmy brought our steed under control short of the drop off. Out we jumped running to the crash. The dust was settling, and the officer was okay standing alongside his wrecked car. The suspect, a drunk female, was dazed but unhurt. We scooped her up, put her in our car, and began trying to maneuver out of the made-for-Hollywood movie set. Spread out before us, we saw what must have been twenty police cars with lights flashing. Officers were everywhere. A lone unit among them was a Salt River Indian police car whose jurisdiction we were on. That could mean *feds*—we didn't want any part of that, so when the Indian police officer indicated he wanted custody of our drunk, we said, "Oh no! She is wanted for felonies back in Phoenix." We roared out of there before he could process this. Traveling back to Phoenix, the drunk female told us she was just having fun and liked the attention she had gotten. We transported her back to the original offending district, wrote our supplement reports, and bid adieu. We got our butts chewed big-time. "How dare you leave the district in a pursuit? I should blah blah blah."

"A, did we say we were in pursuit? B, did we apprehend a felon? C, do you want us to pour the spilled milk back in the bottle?" This supervisor walked away scratching his head.

Looking for something to do

Finding something to do, hmmm …

Jimmy and I often would park our cruiser when radio was slow. We would wander around the alleys and abandoned buildings check-ing for crimes afoot. Translation, we were bored.

One such time we had spotted a john making a deal with a local street lady. We put our Sneaky Pete senses to work, so off we went, following the couple back into the darkened buildings. It only took us a matter of minutes to lose them. "Now what?" Jimmy said. "Stop, wait listen." We could hear a sound we couldn't identify. Following the noise, we found our twosome completing their business behind an abandoned building. Oh, the sound we heard turned out to be the slurping sound as she was blowing him. Snatched 'em up off to jail for indecent exposure. Yes, I know who could possibly be offended by this act.

CHAPTER 10

The Mysterious Mr. Rogers

The time was 1982–1983. I had completed a stint as a counselor at the Phoenix Police Regional Academy and was back working shift 3 on EVB. Upon finishing my assignment at the academy, I had been approached by several lieutenants to begin preparing myself to follow the promotional process and go for sergeant. I knew I had made a difference in the lives and, hopefully, the careers of the recruits. As a counselor, I had acted as their sergeant for eighteen weeks. I knew I could handle the job of Sergeant, but did I want to do that to myself? I was thirty-nine and still full of beans. A night of wild car chases, big fights, and lots of arrests was followed by beer drinking and hopefully some female companionship, as was the norm.

The contacts we had with victims and foes alike brought us often to County Hospital. The staff, mostly females, became interested in the drama behind the stories of the victims we brought them. A natural requirement to unwind would find all of us at an early open bar drinking and telling stories. Of course, after some time, pairs began to form. The group would break up around 10:00 a.m., head home, and do it all over again the next shift. Was I ready to give this up? Supervisors weren't encouraged to socialize with their squads. Our core group consisted of about six to eight nurses and six to eight cops. Just unwinding, nothing rowdy or dangerous. Laurie Rogers, the chief nurse at County's emergency room, was a great gal and part of our group. She announced her husband, Doug, would be moving to Arizona to take a position as a highway patrol supervisor. We had learned through Laurie he was working a similar position with the Minnesota Highway Patrol. A lateral transfer was to happen. First, small doubt—Phoenix PD wouldn't do that, but who knew how the politically driven Arizona DPS worked?

A few weeks later, Mr. Rogers was introduced to the group and became another cog in the wheel of our little social group.

Time and justice marched on, with drinking taking up most mornings. Our little group had now migrated to people's homes to avoid the expenses of bars along with the conversation being overheard by the wrong ears. The first time at Laurie and Doug's house, he made a point of showing his awards, uniforms, and his badge. Moment of doubt number 2: It wasn't necessary to show off this stuff to other cops. If he was to be working undercover, as he had described, why the need for uniforms? Puzzling but not alarming to our fast and furious group. During working hours, several of our police group would use the back room at Coco's restaurant to eat or do paperwork. One evening around 2:00 a.m., Mr. Rogers showed up, asking to join us there. He went on to explain his undercover, was deep under the radar. Hush-hush operation he was involved in was a kiddie porn ring, etc. Well, that was way out of our wheelhouse and sphere of influence, so little attention was given to the story. As time went on, he became quite interested in our department's policies. Nothing unusual—we considered it cops talking. He told stories of his past as a Montana Highway patrol officer. In trying to get hired by Minnesota, they required him to go undercover as an inmate at their Stillwater Prison. He plied us with tales of heroics inside the jail, fighting off inmates' advances with only a mop handle. He never finished with the outcome story of this adventure. He said he was now working, though on loan, with Arizona Department of Public Safety. We found him to be slightly off queue, but his best favorable asset was being married to Laurie. An incident late at night while dining at Coco's gave me pause. Doug had arrived somewhat disturbed and was very fidgety explaining he had an important sting operation going on out at one of the many abandoned airstrips in the desert. Hmm, why was he not there? We were advised by radio that our sergeant was en route to join us for coffee. His location told us he was ten to fifteen minutes away. Doug held his radio's earpiece close and acknowledge a call saying, "Got to go, it's going down." Quite a hasty exit indeed.

A few weeks later, me, my girlfriend, Robin, Laurie, and Doug went up to spend a weekend at my cabin. Laurie was preparing for an important medical exam, and Doug was going along to help her study. It was a good weekend with them two posing questions back and forth. Doug was right more often than not. In the past, he had mentioned working as an EMT while in Montana. The guy's medical knowledge was good.

Doug was one for giving gifts. It was around Christmas, and I had mentioned being broke, unable to get presents for my kids who were living with their mother. It had been my choice to leave, but supporting two families was a bit more than I made. I had picked up a couple of off-duty jobs, and Doug came around with a couple of brand new four-inch buck knives I could have for twenty bucks. Normally about a fifty dollars' value. Didn't think much about where he got them. Over the next few months, I bought a couple of hand-guns and some police equipment from him after he explained they were surplus.

We partied with Doug and his wife, Laurie, often, and all seemed right with the world. Around February 1983, I got a call to report to IA (internal affairs), which no one wanted to visit. I was escorted into an office and told to relax; I wasn't the object of any investigation. A squad mate, Tommy S., a real good street cop, was being investigated for fraternizing with underage girls. Tommy was a good-looking single officer with a fine reputation on the street. The detective pulled out a Polaroid photo of Tommy in a swimming pool surrounded by three topless girls that appeared to be very young. "Have you ever seen this photo before?" I was asked.

"No, I haven't."

"Were you present when a conversation by Tommy about how teenage girls dressed scantily took place?"

"Yeah, I guess."

"Do you recall Tommy say something to the effect that the way they dress it's no wonder they get in trouble. Specifically, have you seen the way they dress?"

"Well, I did remember the conversation and wish I hadn't."

"Your group runs with some of the staff at County Hospital, right?"

"We know who was present during that conversation but can't seem to locate a DPS Lt. Doug Rogers."

"Do you know how to contact him?"

I didn't. I suggested, "Why don't you call DPS?"

"We did, they never heard of this guy. He doesn't work for them." Doug had said some time back if anyone looked for him, DPS would claim ignorance.

"Enough already." I asked, "What has this have to do with me?"

My resistance wasn't appreciated, and they immediately began their typical bullying. "Do you want to be part of this investigation?"

"Seems like I am."

They left the room, followed shortly by the lieutenant for the division Jim H. entering. I respected and trusted him, having dealt with him on prior occasions. "Tom, we are trying to get to the bottom of a very sticky incident, not trying to piss you off."

I said, "Then get rid of your goons who think the cops are their bad guys."

Jim smiled and waved my comment off. "Tommy is a friend of yours?"

"Yep, and a damn fine cop, sir."

"I know, but this incident is very bad and will probably bring him down. You're not involved in it, so keep your distance from it." He left, and I was told I could go. That night, as our shift started, Tommy was absent, and the rumor mill cranked up.

The gist of the story was Tommy had thrown (not physically) his "on again, off again" girlfriend out of his house after discovering a huge phone bill she hadn't paid. The long-distance calls had been to one of her old boyfriends. She got pissed and went to IA with a Polaroid, showing Tommy what turned out to be Tommy with thirteen-year-old topless girls in a swimming pool. Tommy had sworn to IA the incident was years ago; the girls were fooling around and had taken off their tops to embarrass him. Nothing, no touching, had happened. His ex-girlfriend must have found the picture to use it for blackmail. Reasonable explanation but too damaging to survive; he was given an option to resign without his Arizona peace officer status being canceled. He took it, and they wished him well. In the meantime, IA was still wanting to talk to the now very mysterious Mr. Rodgers on the original conversation regarding the scantily dressed teenagers. Rodgers had disappeared. I was called to the captain's office for a chat.

"Did you buy or receive anything from a Doug Rogers?"

"Yeah, I bought some stuff." Well, it turned out he wasn't a DPS lieutenant or any kinda law officer at all. *What!*

Holy shit, this could go sideways fast. We had talked about police work and sensitive issues in his presence. Where did all of his badges, ID cards, and DPS gear come from? This could get ugly if the stuff he sold me was stolen. Everyone involved in any purchases/gifts were directed to run checks for stolen items. Everything I had showed negative results. I, along with other officers from our circle, were told to put anything connected to Rogers in our lockers and keep it there until otherwise advised. The next day, at home, I get a call from Doug. He was real stressed out, wanting to know if IA had contacted me. He claimed he was deep undercover with DPS and our IA wouldn't be told of him by his people. He tried to convince me he was legit and wanted to meet. I told him the only meeting we would have would be for me to arrest him for impersonating an officer. He still tried to protest his innocence as he hung up. My girlfriend, Robin, Laurie's best friend, came to my place. I was feeling pissed at being duped and started into Laurie. She had been crying and looked me right in the eye, asking, "How could I have been so stupid?"

DPS had come to her house looking for Doug, who had already packed and was gone. They had been married in Minnesota prior to her move to Phoenix to take the head ER nurse's job. She thought him to be employed by MGI (Minnesota General Investigations), that state's law enforcement branch. She swore she had seen IDs and a badge for the office. This was a familiar tale to us, also having seen his IDs and badges. I believed her and I could empathize with her. The girls left to stay at Robin's for safety. We didn't know what would happen as the trap for him was tightening. Back at IA, what I had thought would be some serious investigating never materialized. Just leave the stuff in your locker in case they want to look at it; otherwise, it was business as usual. Very strange indeed till word leaked down that Lieutenant Mike J. and his girlfriend, Monica A., one of the ER nurses, had also socialized with Doug and Laurie on many occasions. Furthermore, the lieutenant had bought an assault rifle from Doug at a very reduced rate. Now if this hard-charging upcoming lieutenant was fooled, what could you expect from lowly street cops?

A month later, the Phoenix newspaper broke the story of the phantom DPS Lt. Doug Rogers. His involvement with Phoenix PD was listed as minimum, the real story was shocking enough. He was an ex-con from Minn. He had served time for fraud and assault and was reported to be working with Minnesota's version of the mob. He had been connected to gangland-style killings and was wanted back there for various crimes. I guessed his story about using the mop handle to protect himself was the only true thing he ever said.

The question of how he deposited the correct amounts of money in their joint checking account was never totally answered. The investigation found he was working as a security guard at some of the offices used by DPS, which could explain where some of his IDs came from. They found unexplained loss of petty cash from many of the offices he patrolled. The badges turned out to have been stolen from John's Uniforms, a local place for cops to shop. Rogers often hung out there per the owners. "Yes, thinking about it he was always around when stuff came up missing," John remembered. He recalled Doug even helping them look for a lost DPS lieutenant's badge once. *Bingo!*

It was also discovered many holsters, belt, and uniform shirts were missing. This all added to pieces of the puzzle but never explained the amount of cash he was making. Word leaked back after he was arrested in Minnesota; he had wanted to make sure the Arizona authorities knew that no Arizona cops were involved in his schemes. Six months later, I asked what we should do with the stuff we had put in our lockers. Oh, if anything has serial numbers, check them; otherwise, do what you want with it. Well, that had all been done many months back, Einstein.

Thus the tale of the mysterious Mr. Doug Rogers ended.

CHAPTER 11

More Random Stories of Life on the Street

Can noise be really quiet?

On occasion, it could be really slow. No fugitives to look for, no calls for service, just nothing happening. Since our squad wasn't too good about relaxing, we soon would find a way to break the silence. One such night, our Sergeant Roger K was hanging out at the radio room downtown. To mess with us, 'cause he knew we were at County Hospital's ER hanging out, he had radio clear us to take a call. We had portables, so we could be anywhere answering, right?

"Check the noise disturbance, Twenty-Fourth Street and Washington, no further information."

"10-4." Okay. We finished our coffee and headed that way. The location was a huge dog boarding kennel. We pulled up; all was quiet ... I advised we were 10-23 (arrived), walked over to the fence, keyed my radio talk mic, and said, "It's all quiet here" while rattling my flashlight up and down the chain links. The uproar from hundreds of dogs barking at once was deafening. I held the mic open for five seconds.

Without missing a beat, radio said, "10-4."

Great gag, right? Maybe another ten seconds went by when the on-duty lieutenant (new to the streets) wanted our location for a 10-45 (meet).

He was so mad the veins in his neck stuck way out. He had spittle on his lips and was fumbling over his ass, chewing words. "Who do you think … I'll have your … if you ever …" We tried to explain the humor but were cut short by radio clearing lieutenant to set up a 10-45 with our sergeant. The lieutenant parted with veiled threats of ending our careers. Get a grip, Lieutenant. I guess, as Sergeant K would never tell us, he explained to the lieutenant that it was okay to have a laugh sometimes. Maybe not.

Lieutenant transferred back downtown where he belonged. Comes to mind another slow night. Newly promoted Lieutenant Mike J. requested a 10-45 with us. He was downtown, which was somewhat strange, as it was late and we hadn't screwed up yet that day, so "What's up?" We were riding the far eastern beat, which included Papago Park. Assuming he knew, we lodged an arrow we had found earlier into our light bar. After all, our beat was known as Indian Country. We headed to his location and pulled up slowly for all to see.

He started to ask a question when he saw the arrow and said, "Never mind, I can see you have been busy," and drove off. He had a CO (civilian observer) in the car, who was laughing his ass off. Would have given anything to have been a little fly in that car.

Some of the Characters of EVB

I was doing paperwork in my car one night near Twenty-Fourth Street and East Van Buren. A station wagon full of kids with Mom and Pop pulled up and asked if they could have a word with me. Certainly, see, it wasn't often we were contacted by regular folks. Pound for pound, East Van Buren had more hookers, pimps, addicts, drug dealers, and general degenerates than anywhere in our world. The family's story—they had pulled into a motel nearby to spend the night. Paid the fee and took the kids to the room. "The place was real cute, it had rooms kinda like log cabins."

"Do you know what they were showing on the TV?"

"Yep, I do."

The Log Cabin Motel, in its prime, probably was very popular with families but now was a "no-tell motel" complete with full-blown porn. Well, it didn't seem fair for the clerk to have rented them a room. I told them to follow me. Arrived back at the sleazy place, and we went inside to right this wrong.

"So sorry, can no refund money. He pay go way."

"Wrong answer, shit bird. Either they get their money back or I will sit with my fully marked police car in your driveway all night and many nights to come. It will be my new favorite place to park every night. Got it?"

He did, and a refund of their money happened. Sometimes you have to explain things in a way that is understood. Ma and Pa were so grateful, thanking me over and over. I watched them and the kiddies wave goodbye, smiling to myself.

A very young prostitute approached me one evening and asked for a moment of my time. "What can I do for you, my love?" Seemed a few days before a customer, having completed his business, had given her a check for services rendered. Problem was, it wasn't honored by the bank NSF. "Let me see it." Sure enough, the address and phone number was on it. Hmmmmm. I guess you could visit his home or call and ask (hopefully his wife) to make good on the check. A picture of this happening came to my mind. Just doing my public service. Again, to be a little fly watching that outcome. Yes, I did advise her, her business was usually cash and carry only.

There were many characters known to us working the EVB area. Some come to mind as I write this.

Jamie J. was one. Jamie, a Mexican, was about twenty, small in stature, and a big-time cross dresser. He pulled tricks for a living but mostly stayed away from EVB. I wandered up to Thomas Road, our northern boundary, having heard a call for extra units at the scene of a serious pedestrian accident. The location was one of our "clubs" that catered to all sorts of the odd elements of society. Arriving at the scene, I found an assortment of emergency vehicles parked in various locations, causing a "Lookie Lou" traffic jam. Fire/rescue was working on the victim, whom I recognized as Jamie. Listening, I heard a fireman say, "I can't get a heartbeat."

Pausing a moment, I suggested if he removed Jamie's falsies, it might help.

"Awwwww, shit" was the reply as the fluffy add-ons went flying. Jamie was scrapped and bruised but otherwise okay.

Several weeks later, we spotted Jamie on EVB. I contacted him and reminded he/she/shim would be wise to leave the area.

"It's a free country," was his answer.

"Yes, yes, it is."

"But not free to commit your illegal activities." We drove off, appearing to leave the area but instead finding a location where we could keep an eye on him. Shortly, a pickup truck complete with a cowboy, Stetson and all, pulled up. Jamie jumped in, and off they went. We waited, knowing he would return soon since he never used a room to conduct business. Ten minutes later, just like clockwork, up pulled the cowboy and his truck. Jamie jumped out, blowing Tex a kiss. The truck drove away, and we followed it for a mile or so. We lit him up and made the stop.

"Is there a problem, officers?"

I looked away from him and said, "Officer Jim, I told you this guy doesn't look gay."

"That you did, Officer Fribbs, that you did."

"What?"

"I'm no fucking queer, why did you think that?" He was real indignant now, all puffed up.

"Well, we wondered why you would pick up a fag to have sex with."

"No! No way, man, she was a girl."

"Really, did you feel anything a girl has?"

That look of recognition which comes when one goes "Oh crap" appeared on his face. "You mean that was a guy?" I could see him going over the recent encounter in his mind. A very dark picture was emerging. We ran him for wants and warrants with negative results. Actually, we were legitimizing the stop.

Knowing we had made his day, "You are free to go, sir," was our departing comment. We got a series of radio calls and answered them then raced back to our hiding spot, but no Jamie. Somewhat later, we responded to take a report of an assault call at County Hospital ER. Wouldn't you know it … there was Jamie. One eye closed, a tooth missing from his split lips. He/she/shim was a mess.

"You told him, didn't you?"

"Why, Jamie, whatever are you talking about?"

Needless to say, he didn't want a report made about what had happened to him after his illegal actions. Street justice was served.

While I ran into Jamie from time to time over the years, I never saw him/she/shim on EVB again.

From the Shades of *Grapes of Wrath*

The HillBilly's Incident

Once in a while, you would run into a situation that just amazed and amused at the same time.

We were dispatched to a loud disturbance NFI (no further information). It only took one time in your career to ask dispatch, "Is there any more information on this call?"

"If I knew more, you would too!" response corrected your ignorance. The Pear was driving, of course (said I'd fall asleep so I wasn't allowed to drive) as we headed to the location. It was early in the morning, must have been winter, as we had jackets on. The site of the call, a rundown collection of one and two story shacks had recently become the waypoint for a new wave of *Grapes of Wrath* folks migrating to Cal-e-for-ni-a. They were the source of at least a few disturbance calls every night. We didn't have a numbered address, which wouldn't have helped anyway. Just follow your ears to the problem. Yelling and some screaming led us farther into the cluster of buildings. Behold, a male, female, and small child standing below a staircase. The adults were midtwenties, him with long greasy hair and a scraggly beard. She was short and round, putting in mind a Christmas tree bulb. The bundled-up half-asleep child was being held by her.

Jethro (I'll call him) was yelling to the area above the staircase, "Daddy, I want my mink oil. It's mine, I want it now."

It startled him when we walked up behind him and said, "Shut up."

"Ohhh, am I glad you're here."

"Really? Then why didn't you call for service instead of babbling out here like an idiot? Now in your very best quiet voice, tell us what is the problem." Sounds like how you talk to your children, yeah.

"Okay, okay, but I want my wife (we will call her Ellie May) to start the story. Go ahead, honey." I do not lie. Well, Ellie began to unfold the saga. Seemed his daddy had been living with them during the migration west. One afternoon, Ellie found Grandpa taking a bath with his three-year-old granddaughter. When confronted, he said she was dirty, so ... Ellie went about her business till Jethro came home.

"Stop! Stop! Let me tell it from here!" Jethro shouted (I had to remind him about his very quiet voice). During this prolonged desertion, Officer Chuck R. had arrived, wondering what was taking so long. Pear and Chuck moved around behind the migrants and began making faces at me while picking their noses. Wasn't bad enough that I could hardly keep a straight face anyway. Jethro was becoming real animated as he continued, "Ellie May told me what happened when I came home, so I asked Daddy what had he done? 'Nothing,' he said, 'the child was dirty, so was I, so we took a bath, so shut up and leave me alone.'" Jethro, now the investigator, wasn't satisfied with this answer. He was now looking at the child his wife was holding. He got real serious, and with a pained look on his face said to the child, "Mary Lou ... did Grandpa touch your pud?"

OMG, pud?

"Yeah, Daddy, he did ..." came the squeaky reply.

Jethro, now renamed Pud Man, explained, "I never say dirty words in front of the child."

This should have been a serious moment, but no, the two baboons that were my backups left holding their sides while I had to maintain. I inquired if he wanted to launch an investigation about this incident. His puzzled look said no. "He made us move out since he was paying the rent, and all I want is my *mink oil*."

What the hell was mink oil? I didn't know, nor did my abandoned partners. Must have been some expensive stuff since minks aren't very big. I briefly suggested the daylight hours might find Daddy more agreeable to the return of the oil. Satisfied, Jethro took one last look up the stairs, cupped his hands around his mouth, and in his loudest hillbilly drawl said, "Daddy ... I told the *secret*" and then departed with his little family.

We didn't have the Internet and Google back then, so I had to search to find out mink oil was a leather preservative. No it didn't come from minks, geeeez. And I thought hillbillies were dumb.

Maybe you had to be there ...

Fun on Zero Dark Thirty (Name for the Overnight Shift)

In most cities, large or small, during the late shift, only a few, if any, restaurants stay open. Remember that if you are a night owl, locate these places in your town 'cause if you are out and want to find a cop, bingo!

We had a small group gathered at the Denny's Thirty-Second Street, East Van Buren. Had to be around 2:00 a.m. Three officers were assembled; surely we were discussing some important police business ... like which waitress would date. Our sergeant's, Issy U's, voice broke through the radio's silence. He was screaming in Spanish something that none of us understood. We heard "Thirty-Second Street, Van Buren something ..." We were at that location, so outside we rushed to find nothing. He continued putting out information in "South of the Border" language; we had no clue what was happening. We split up searching for our lost sergeant. We located him behind some flop house south of Twenty-Fourth Street and EVB. He was holding three black males at gunpoint while yelling at them in Spanish. We scooped them up to their relief. They truly thought he was crazy. The bandits safely tucked in our cars, the story unfolded.

Sgt. Issy U. was sitting in his patrol car at Twenty-Fourth Street and EVB doing some paperwork when he began checking the inside of his eyelids (fell asleep). He awoke to the sounds of people yelling with a cab pulled right in front of his patrol car. The driver was frantic, screaming in tongues of unknown origin. Three black guys were running away to further confuse the scene. Issy, not always the calmest cucumber in the basket, reverted to his native tongue, Spanish, thus his broadcast. Calmer moments explained the event. The three black males had been picked up by the cabbie for a ride. Shortly they produced knives and a gun to relieve him of his money. The cabbie spotted Sgt. Issy's parked marked police car and drove right at it. The robbers, being a tad smarter than the average felon, unassed the cab, but having no idea where they were, ran off together. Always amazed me how two or more suspects always ran off together, which certainly increased our chances of spotting them tenfold.

Thus, Issy found them hiding only a few yards from the scene.

He was puzzled why no one had responded to his initial call for help till it was explained his broadcast was in Spanish. "Oh …" was the only reply.

You see, this had happened a few times before during his career. A great guy who was fun to work for.

An incident attributed to then officer Issy went something like this. He was new and riding with an Old Salt when they responded to a suicidal person at a home. They arrived, and the wife cautioned them the husband was despondent, had a gun, and was held up in a back bedroom. Remember, this was the olden days before SWAT SAU, etc. Issy and Salt went to the room and opened the door to be confronted by the armed man, pointing the gun at them. Issy fired one shot of double aught buck from his twelve-gauge while Salt emptied his six shooter. It was over in seconds as they closed the door. The wife, quite distraught, asked if her husband was okay. "No, he's dead. We killed him," was officer Issy's answer. Don't believe it? I heard the story from the source.

CHAPTER 12

17 South Second Avenue
Stories of the Old Jail

I will try to paint a picture of the Old Jail, located on the upper floors of the then County Courthouse at 17 South Second Avenue. The building was shared with the County Court System and contained our police department's administrative offices (the brass), radio room dispatch, detective bureau, and the jail upstairs. Currently, those offices and bureaus take up several multistory buildings. We avoided this location unless a prisoner was to be booked. To book a suspect, you entered through a side door into the desk sergeant's location. He would peruse your booking slip for errors, then you were on your way. His approval of your arrest and paperwork was necessary to proceed. Having gotten his okay, securing your weapon was required to head upstairs via an elevator. The elevator, which over the years had been the sight of many an attitude adjustment, was small and contained no camera. I saw many an arrestee enter it acting all bad and, after the slow ride up, emerge quite meek. Maybe they passed through a twilight zone or a knee to the nuts had adjusted their behavior. A few steps and you were at the booking area. Again your paperwork was checked while a few questions were asked of your prisoner. "Are you injured?" "Do you know why you are here?" "Do you have any medical issues we should know about?" It didn't seem to matter what the response was. Every subject, unless the charges were felonies, went into one large cell prior to being sorted out for court or release.

Let that sink in. You just got arrested on a warrant for that over-due library book you forgot about five years ago. You are in the same cell as the vagrant that has pissed and shit all over himself. "Howdy stranger, what you in for?" he asks. Picture a TV documentary show-ing hundreds of walruses or seals all clinging to a rock; that would be the sight of the drunk tank on a weekend night. One open urinal for maybe one hundred guys. Regulars would grab a mattress as they were sent inside while first timers would cling to the bars, await-ing rescue (bailed out). I often thought if a night in the drunk tank didn't alter your behavior, nothing could. While I worked as a reserve officer, prior to going regular, I often worked at the jail to assist pro-cessing prisoners. In the booking area were two steel poles the pris-oner was directed to grab hold of while spreading their legs prior to being searched. Though they were to have been totally searched and their property stowed prior to ever being here, stuff was always being found. Case in point—I was doing a search when I put my hand into this miscreant's back pocket to feel oozing through my fingers. My first thought was he had shit his pants. I nearly up chucked right there as I withdrew a half-eaten burrito. The turd got mad when I threw it in the trash can. The old-timers got a chuckle out of it.

While waiting for his processing, Cowboy sitting on the bench announced, "You all want my boots off, you all will have to take 'um off."

The flurry of officers that headed to assist him surprised me.

The booking sergeant said "Stop" to the gathered officers. "I will help this young fellow remove his footwear." Up came Tex's leg while he smirked. Sergeant grabbed the boot while shoving his own size 12 into stupid's crotch. He pulled and pushed while standing on the guy's balls, but the darn boot just wouldn't come off. The ensu-ing scream startled some of the drunks and rose in decibels as Sarge continued helping remove the stuck boot. Finally removing one boot he was asked if he would need help with the other one. His tearful response was a quiet *no.* Yes, there were cameras in locations through-out the buildings, but they never seemed to be in a spot to catch the action. Hmmmmmmm …

CHAPTER 13

Communications Center and
Radio Dispatch Room

Until the new police and public safety building was completed around 1979–1980, 17 South Second Avenue was the headquarters for the Phoenix Police Department. Thus the location of the next story.

All incoming calls for service were routed through here. The radio room which dispatched the calls was also located next to it. A call would come into the operators, who would decide if it warranted an officer response. If so, a small card was filled out with the particulars, then put on a conveyor belt, which carried it into the radio room. These two rooms were separated by a glass-walled partition. So ... call comes in; operators fill out a card that goes to the radio room by a conveyor belt where a supervisor routed it to the radio operator for that district. Sounds simple enough. The wrinkle comes when some of the phone operators are officers on light or modified duty (might have been recovering from injuries, etc.) who tend to get bored easily. I'll describe one such night. Officer X, who will remain unnamed, was working the phones while his broken leg healed. He took a call from a female reporting a man in a high-rise window across from her window was exposing himself. Officer X filled out the request for services card, writing something similar to what the caller had told him. He chuckled to himself as the little card traveled down the conveyor belt. As it neared entry into the radio room, he thought, *Oops, I better not be fooling around.* He tried to get up to chase down the card, but his immobile leg caused him to tip over in his chair. He was now tangled up in his chair as he saw the card disappear into the radio room. Oh no! It was past the point of recovering it. The radio supervisor snatched up the card and efficiently passed it to the district operator while Officer X now on his feet watched and listened through the window.

"928 ... see the woman 1234 N. Central apartment 20 reference man in a window choking his chicken." Radio rarely was ever silent, but the airways went dead for several seconds until microphones began clicking (cops' way of laughing). While this officer became a legend in his own time, I heard he enjoyed a few days at home without pay for the incident. No sense of humor I guess.

Civilian Observer Ride Along

Working late shift out of old Sky Harbor Precinct when it came my turn to take a CO on a ride along. CO (civilian observer) were allowed by the department to ride with the police to observe life as seen by an officer working the streets. No big deal, except every cop I ever knew hated it. It just cramped your style since being half paranoid, you didn't know if they might be an IA (internal affairs) plant. The assignment process was rotated unless the sarge was pissed at you. My turn was up, and I went out to the lobby to meet my Shadow for the evening. Turned out to be two, a father and son. This changed plans, as our squads had a screen separating the back seat from the driver. This would have caused one of them to sit back in the prisoner's compartment. I had to find a unit without a shield. I solved the issue by taking a sergeant's car that didn't use shields. It also had a shotgun rack that was absent from regular units. The father was about seventy to seventy-five with his son much younger. I took them on the obligatory tour of the station. Not much going on as it was early. Out to our MOP (mobile operating platform) and we hit the bricks. Always the first questions from a CO: "Are you married? Kids? Where did you come from?" etc. They were really curious about who you were and why police work. I ran through the litany of standard answers till it came to being from Ottawa, Illinois.

Senior's jaw dropped, and when he said, "Well, we are too," mine dropped.

Imagine the odds of this encounter. It got weirder as we talked. "Who is your dad?"

"Well, he's dead, but his name was Albert Fribbs."

"Moppie, you're Moppie's kid?"

I had to pull off the road to absorb this. I'll digress back to the early forties when my dad was in his thirties. Senior knew of him during that time. Dad's handle (nickname) came from the slow way he walked and talked. He was 6'4" and thin. I was really taken back as I knew only a few stories of my father as related by family. I was three when he died. We talked about Ottawa and growing up there having a great time between calls. It truly is a very small world indeed.

The Duce and the Tootsie Roll

Gary, my older brother by two years, often rode with me as a CO. The department, at that time, encouraged this to help family members understand the life we were leading. I say "at that time" 'cause some years later, a lieutenant, trying to impress and maybe gain favors of a couple of pretty girls who were riding with him, nearly killed them. Lieutenant went racing up Central Avenue to an in-progress call and promptly ran head-on into a large palm tree. Totaled the car and sent everyone to the ER.

It was a rather quiet Sunday morning as Gary and I cruised the downtown area. Downtown Phoenix consisted mainly of financial and law enforcement buildings. The fourteen blocks by six block area on Monday through Friday, eight to five, was a hub of activity. After 5:00 p.m., a metamorphosis took place. Bordering the south of downtown was the produce area, so named for the vegetables, etc. that were bought and sold there. After the good people of the business area took leave of the area, the creatures of the night began to appear. All sorts of miscreants began popping up to populate the sidewalks, alleys, and doorways.

The Duce would come alive. Its name was either short for *Produce* or for the once two block area is formerly covered. Known in other cities as Skid Row or the Barrio, it was a great place for a new officer to work or be trained. Allow me to back up a bit. As a rookie reserve officer, I was given the delightful opportunity to work this area with veteran officers during my early training. What an eye-opening experience. Officers John D. and Doug W., just to mention a few, liked me and took me under their wings. The area was covered by walking beat officers. (Read Joseph Wambaugh's *The Blue Knight* for a great read on street life in Skid Row.) I suspect a human waste magnet must have been turned on after five that drew the city's lowest forms to this area. Seven blocks long, seven blocks wide suddenly as alive as an ant colony. Prostitutes, addicts, Indians, Mexicans and everyone drunk or working on it. We had a law that said if you were drunk in the public, you could be considered a danger to yourself or others thus you needed to go to jail. Short and sweet. The paperwork took about two minutes, and the lawbreaker would be put in a roaming paddy wagon. When the wagon was full, off it went to the jail located a few blocks away. Really, we tried to keep these people from killing themselves or each other. Life's value could be the price of a bottle of wine. Failure to share might get you opened up with a straight razor. We walked around, keeping eyes on known trouble spots. There were only five bars and two places to eat, so the four walking teams usually kept things under control.

On one lovely evening, I was walking with John D. as we approached the Busy Bee Cafe, when out the door rushed a drunk whom you thought must be on fire; he was running as fast as his wobbly legs could manage while looking back over his shoulder. At that moment, Officer Harry H. pulled up on his Harley-Davidson police motorcycle and said, "You want him?"

John said, "Yeah." Harry took off down the sidewalk on the Hog, caught up, and kicked him into a parking meter. The crumpled quivering mass of protoplasm was still breathing as he lay on the pavement. We walked into the bee and asked what the guy that ran out had done. We were met with silence. Nobody knew anything about him or his hasty exit.

Busy Bee Cafe
(located in the heart of the Duce)

Ooooops. We checked him out and asked if he wanted to go home or jail. He chose home, and we got a beat car to transport him. And the beat goes on. Occasionally, the Duce would produce (no pun intended) a true evil creature. This would cause us real trouble.

Beat Car
Mobile Operating Platform (MOP)

The Duce drunks were being stabbed while they lay in their booze-induced comas. A few had died, and the press had picked up the story. A scheme to catch the perp was devised. We would use an undercover officer as a decoy. Officer Wil T., our full-blood Hopi Indian, volunteered and got dressed for the charade. He looked and smelled the part, having poured twenty-twenty Mad Dog wine on himself. We located a spot where we could watch him and waited. Wil was curled up in a doorway with the rest of his twenty-twenty bottle exposed. The waiting began. First couple of insects just took drinks from his bottle. A stakeout officer was sent to get more wine to supplement our setup. Soon, a huge, menacing-looking creature approached. He was doing the suspect look around so we knew we were about to have trouble. After searching through Wil's pockets he brought out a knife, and he tried to stab him. The stakeout team was on him instantly. He was beaten soft before the detectives arrived to question him. Wil was cut but only needed a butterfly bandage. Officer Wil T., a former Marine, had served two tours in Vietnam and had been wounded seriously but found this injury minor. Wil became a legend in his own time when this undercover operation became known for police generations to come as the Tootsie Roll.

It was undetermined if our guy was the stalker, so the operation continued with other decoys until one night, in a struggle with one of the robbers, Officer John D. accidentally shot him. John had grabbed the struggling guy and was pushing him up against a wall, when his gun, which was in his other hand, went off. That was the same action involved in my shoot-a-wall incident. A later review found police officers being taught to keep their finger off the trigger to avoid this happening. The powers to be got their collective heads together and decided the stalker must certainly have been caught or scared off, and the days of the Tootsie Roll were over.

Now that you have an image of the Duce in your mind, we'll get back to my brother and I riding on a Sunday morning in the Duce. *Beeeeeeep*—hot tone. "Aggravated assault in progress." It was a few blocks away where the suspect, using a baseball bat, had battered some fool's head. Figuring which way the turd would run, I turned the corner to find him running while he looked behind him, perfect as he flew head over heels across my car's hood. I was out in an instant, planting him back on the hood, and cuffed him. I called for the unit that had the original call and turned him over. Total time consumed about ten minutes. Gary was awed. Sometimes you just get lucky.

Wrong Car, Right Guy

Luck and instinct combined are powerful police officer's tools. Working late shift out of old Sky Harbor Station with an academy cadet when a 211 just occurred in the area of 40 ST and East Van Buren was broadcast. We were a long way off but started that direction. Arriving units on the scene broadcast a suspect and vehicle description as we continued east on Van Buren. A somewhat unusual vehicle description had the getaway car with a large dent in the driver's side door. As if by magic, the next car passing us the other way had a molded continental kit built onto the trunk. This gave the appearance of a dent/deformity. Could this be what the victim saw? I whipped a U-turn, pulling in behind this car, and lit it up. The driver made a furtive motion, pushing something under the passenger's seat. The car pulled to the curb without hesitation. We advised radio of our location with a possible suspect and approached the car. I wasn't totally convinced we had the right guy as it wasn't unusual for people to try to hide things when being stopped. I contacted the driver who sat motionless and saw a knit watch hat and part of a paper bag sticking out from under the passenger's seat.

I asked, "Do you know why I stopped you?"

"Yes, sir. I'm sorry. I just needed the money."

Well, there you go. It was the right guy. The money in the paper bag along with his gun were recovered from under the front seat. We promptly hooked him up and stowed him in our patrol car. We headed back to the scene, an all-night "no tell" motel with the rookie driving the suspect's car. We would get him ID'd and haul him off to jail. I have to say I was feeling pretty smug about this catch and my ability to figure it out.

At the scene, the suspect was immediately identified. I said, "That's the car, right?" pointing at the car my rookie had driven there.

"Nope, that's not the car. His car had a big dent in the door like I told the other officers."

What? All my brilliant intuitive work and really Lady Luck caught him. The suspect was an airman from Luke Air Force Base who had serious money problems. I don't know what happened to him after we booked him with a hold for the Air Police.

Bush Whacking

Sometimes officers would get into problems even if their intentions were basically okay. Papago Park is a city park connected to the Phoenix Zoo. After closing, the sprawling acreage was often the choice for lovers to park and neck, etc. The beat car for the park was responsible for running them off. Trouble started when a far-too-anxious officer wanted to sneak a peek at the usually undressed female participant. Now this wasn't Peeping Tom work, just a flash-light turned on as the couple was rousted. It was referred to as *bush whacking*. Mostly, the offending couple was given an opportunity to dress, names taken, and sent on their way with a warning. Sounds harmless, right? The problem came when Miss Sweetness went home thinking maybe her folks might find out what happened. She would spout a tale about how she, a fifteen-year-old, had been forced by her eighteen-year-old boyfriend to do the horizontal mambo. Now we have a felony committed in the officer's presence without an arrest. Daddy wanted something done about this, and the cop was hang-ing out a mile. The lying girl would get out the truth when it was pointed out her lover would be bunking with large horny black men if she stuck to her story. Even the cry of statutory rape disappeared when Daddy's little angel would need to testify in open court. It was best to shine your spotlight, hit the siren, and make lots of noise prior to contacting the consenting couples. The best answer was to avoid the problem.

Really Dumb Criminals

Criminals as depicted in shows like *Cops, Rookie Blues*, etc., often look really dumb. I'm here to tell you many are. Following are a few examples. After pulling over a car weaving virtually curb to curb, the driver would deny having had anything to drink. Through bloodshot eyes, a slurred-speaking driver would try to convince you of their sobriety. "I only heading home ahserfer." The smell coming from them and the car was akin to a brewery spill.

I wondered if they in their pickled mind thought we would say, "Oh well, in that case please forgive me for bothering you, sir." Yet they would seemed surprised as you removed them from their two-thousand-pound instrument of deathly force. Drunks kill far more people than all the guns, but it isn't on purpose. Yeah, tell that to the victims and their families.

We responded to an armed robbery that had just occurred at a Circle K Market out on E. Van Buren Street. The suspect was gone when we arrived and a wallet was lying on the counter. "You're kidding me, right?"

"Nope, it's his, he left it!"

The ID in it was the robber, and his address was right around the corner.

"Let's go hook him up," was my reply. We did.

He answered the door with a "Can I help you, Officer?"

We said "No!" as we spun him around, locking the silver bracelets on.

He began his denial with, "I didn't rob that K. I was at home." Really, who said anything about a robbery slick? Off to the Grey Bar Motel goes another "never to be a brain surgeon."

Similarly, a burglar, when surprised by an early returning homeowner, dove out a window of the house, which caused his wallet to fall on the floor. A quick trip to the suspect's house as provided from the wallet ID and another one bites the dust.

Officer Ricky R. went code 6 (traffic stop) with a vehicle. I was close, so I swung by to make this backup. It appeared he was having an animated conversation with the driver. I pulled up, and I hurried to his side to find him, pulling the driver out of the van. It had happened very quickly with the driver now on the ground. The problem came up when we discovered the guy's legs didn't work. Yep, he was a paraplegic with special controls for his van. The trouble began when he ran a red light in front of Ricky and then refused to pull over when the lights were put on him. After finally stopping, he became a prick, not wanting to show his driver's license. It was somewhat embarrassing as we talked to him sitting on the ground. He was beginning to realize the hole he was digging for himself. I was thinking about the paperwork ahead of us for pulling this poor defenseless cripple out of the car, blah blah … Cooler heads now decided, with our assistance, he reentered his truck, apologized for his behavior and went on his way. Why you say didn't we make this fool pay for his transgressions. The explanation needed for pulling a paraplegic out of his truck, coupled with the requirements to get him checked out at the hospital prior to booking him, was too great. Enough said?

CHAPTER 14

Pranks Can Go Wrong

Officer Byron G, an up-and-coming hard-charging officer, had just bought a brand-new Harley-by-God-Davidson Motorcycle. Real pretty sportster. He brought it to work, parking it under the motor's shed. This area was reserved for police motorcycles only. We all looked at it as we arrived for work, noting he was so proud. After briefing was over, some of us decided a little prank was in order. We pulled out several oil dip sticks from the cars around and dripped the oil under his bike. In years past, Harleys were known to leak oil. The plan called for all of us to reassemble when we got off work to watch his reaction. Well, "the best-laid plans of mice and men," as the saying goes. We, all except Byron, got held over with calls. The next night, he told us the results. When he saw the oil, he went ape shit. He rode immediately to the dealership and demanded a new bike and anybody's ass that was in his way. He raged as they tried to prove there were no leaks. A threat to call the police to have him removed finally settled him down. They simply could not give an explanation for the appearance of the oil. Yes, he was very pissed at us when we unveiled the truth.

A story relayed to me by a very good friend and officer, Don F. needs to be told. Don, a seasoned officer, was patrolling near downtown when the hot tone advised of an armed robbery that had just occurred at First National Bank on South Central. You make a choice at this point: do I go to the scene or look for the bandit? His decision was made for him as the described getaway car drove past him.

Don took up the chase, and the driver pulled over. He shouted for the driver to show his hands which he didn't. The suspect sat in the car without moving. Not responding to Don's commands left little choice but to approach the car. Two methods were taught over the years. Stay close to the car when approaching to minimize the angle he could shoot at you or make a wide arc so as to be able to see his hand movements. Don choose the latter, moving in an arc away from the car. The suspect reached for the gun on the seat next to him and began raising it. Don fired as this was happening. The suspect slumped in the seat. Assured he presented no danger, Don checked for a pulse and found none. Don advised radio of the shooting and waited for the Calvary to arrive.

First on the scene was his sergeant, who asked, "Is he dead?"

"Yep," was Don's answer.

"How many times did you fire?"

"Six."

"How many times did you hit him?"

"Six." Don was always a man of few words. It was later determined the suspect was a career bank robber who had vowed to never go back to prison. I guess you could say he kept his oath.

Another bank robbery is worth telling. Day shift routine patrolling when a hot tone broke the silence: "Bank Robbery just occurred on East Indian School Road." The location was out of our district but I moseyed in that direction. A string of 211s had recently been taking place around our area, and I had a bank surveillance photo from a prior one with me. Radio was advising units were following a possible suspect vehicle west on Indian School. A very good description of the vehicle had been broadcast. We were looking for a late model full-size Ford pickup, extend cab gray over red, with a partial license plate number. This could help to narrow down the search. Not too infrequently, witnesses got mixed up with these sort of things, so I didn't hold all that much confidence in the description. The pursuing units were a long ways off, so on a hunch I began to search parking lots of the motels on Van Buren. Bingo—I spotted a matching vehicle whose license plate, which they had now broadcast, matched. It had been parked so the license plate wasn't showing. I moved my cruiser out of sight and went to the office. A male matching the robbers description had just, five minutes before, checked in. I called for the Calvary and my sergeant to supplement our posse. Having the place surrounded, we called the rooms on either side of the suspect's room and had them quietly leave. We approached the robbers room and had the manager call the room, telling the occupant he was needed outside. Just like in the movies, he opened the door and stepped out with us all over him. We hustled him off to the side, where I took out my previously mentioned photo. Ahhh, it wasn't him. What the heck …

Right truck, just checked in. Well, it wasn't him. By now, we were sure the picture I had was the same guy who had just pulled the robbery today. The fellow we had captured did have an outstanding traffic warrant anyway. He commented we sure went to a lot of fuss over a traffic warrant. I don't think anyone told him differently as he was transported to jail. Checked back with the desk clerk, showing him the robber's photo.

"Oh, that guy, he's in room 205. Checked in yesterday."

We assembled again and went to 205 and knocked, announcing, "Room service."

A voice replied, "I'm not coming out, but you can come in." Sounded like an invitation to a gun fight to me. My Sergeant, another officer and myself took the invite, crashed the door, and charged the suspect. His hands were on his head, and they were quickly cuffed. The weapon was on the nightstand along with the loot from the bank. He admitted his guilt as he explained he didn't want to come out because he thought we would shoot him. He had been robbing banks to support his recently acquired crack cocaine habit. Young fellow who had no criminal record till now. As stated before, sometimes you get lucky.

Not infrequently, supervisors, for entertainment, would follow in on Jimmy and my calls. We were on a family fight at the Theater Motel (so named for the drive-in theater next door). The gist of the call was the Cajun husband was drunk again and verbally abusive. He was a repeat customer who we recently bounced around some before taking him to jail. He had learned from the experience and was very cooperative tonight. In his deep Louisiana accent, he tried to convinces us he was not the ogre his wife was alleging. He was hard to understand, but we didn't really care what he was jabbering, since upon arrival, we quickly knew no crimes had occurred. Newly promoted Lieutenant David B. was observing the dialog while the doofus tried to explain he had only tried to "scale" her "so shid be a gooder wife." I was able to understand about every fourth or fifth word.

Lieutenant wasn't picking up any, and he turned to me and said, "Fribbo, what language is he speaking?"

Without missing a beat, I said, "Mumbo Jumbo."

Lieutenant had to step outside to keep from cracking up completely. We left the now happy couple after I reminded Rube what a trip to jail with us was like. Years later, any time I came in contact socially or otherwise with Lieutenant (later Chief) Dave B., all he had to say was "Mumbo Jumbo?" to crack us up.

CHAPTER 15

Court for Cops

My court appearances were always a source of amusement if not amassment. I'll give you a little primer of the courts. There are two "types" of criminal actions, misdemeanors and felonies, but of course many kinds of crimes. Different kinds of courts are established to handle this array of criminal activity. We'll confine our discussion to misdemeanors and felonies. Issues like minor assault, theft, and shoplifting are misdemeanors and handled in the city or county courts attached to them. Example—shoplifter takes a pack of cigarettes go to the court in the city which it happened. Same guy steals a case of cigarettes valued at over $250, it becomes a felony and he goes to County Court. Same with minor assault goes to city court, major assault off to County Court. Basically, Misdemeanor = City, Felony = County. How do you draw the line between? Very good question to ask. When goods are involved, it usually is by value when humans are involved it is by severity. Misdemeanors can only be punished by up to and can't exceed one year in a county or city jail. If the punishment exceeds one year, then it has to be a felony. I'll throw yet another wrinkle at you—all federal crimes are felonies. So there you go clear as mud.

Fun in Justice of the Peace Court

Felony charges can be placed on a person by the county attorney's office through a Grand Jury indictment. Yes, they really do indict ham sandwiches. County attorneys can also use the Justice of the Peace Courts to bind subject over for trial. Both methods are used. In a grand jury, only the county attorney speaks to the jury with no defense attorney involved. Thus the ham sandwich quote. At JP court, the defense has an opportunity to question, though limited, testimony.

I always wore my Mickey Mouse belt buckle when I wore civilian clothes to court. I was asked only once if I was making a statement about the judicial system. Smile and nod. If you have ever been to court as an officer, witness, or defendant, the contrast between the criminal event and its court presentation are dramatic. Let's say today we're in court for a vehicle manslaughter case. Very serious incident. At the scene—crashed cars, broken glass, broken bodies, blood, sometimes body parts. Emergency vehicles with their red and blue lights flashing parked everywhere, organized chaos. Officers trying to interview witnesses and vehicle drivers. Fireman working on injured people while everyone watches to ensure no one else gets hurt. What had been a normal city street moments before now resembles a war zone. The smell of burning flares engulfs the area.

Flash forward to court. Austere surroundings with everything in its place, a library, quiet throughout the room. *Orderly* would describe this scene. Each participant has a role and a structured place in this play. The Prosecutor always sits in line with the witness stand, and the defense is relegated off to the side. The jurors can be located at different spots depending on the court layout. A court reporter and bailiff round out the staff. Depending on the severity of the charges and or money the defendant has, it will usually determine the number of attorneys present. The state represented by a county attorney will have an investigator and maybe the arresting officer. The court is a very sterile environment to ensure a "fair trial." I was always taken back at the contrast.

In JP court, hearsay evidence is usual admitted as it is a hearing to see if probable cause exists to hold the suspect for trial. Hopefully, I haven't totally confused you.

Back to JP court. Judge Harold L., a somewhat flamboyant figure around the judicial system, was running his JP court. The officer had given his testimony before the defendant's attorney objected to the hearsay evidence given. Judge Harold L. calmly reminded the council they were in a JP court, where it was admissible. This defense attorney, not satisfied, continued his rant about the injustice and sham of the court. From under His Honor's robe, he produced an aerosol can that was labeled Bullshit Spray and sprayed the attorney. The room erupted in laughter and took many minutes to get order restored. The defense attorney did file a formal complaint.

In city court, where I often found myself, a series of short misdemeanor trials were waiting to be heard. Officer tells his story and identifies the suspect; defendant denies everything; judges rules. Next

The officer was on the stand for a prostitution case underway, involving a transvestite. City attorney asked, "Officer, would you identify the defendant in this case for the court?"

"Yes," he said, pointing at the defendant. "It's the guy sitting at the defense table in the pink chiffon dress." A moment's pause was followed by an eruption of laughter that required the judge to call a recess. I rarely was required to go to court for felony trials. Mostly I made sure my cases were solid, which left little room for the defendant to try to wiggle out. Serious charges could bring the case there since the perp had nothing to lose. No plea could be entertained due to the criminal record of the suspect. On one case, I arrived early and went to the court to find the prosecutor, who was studying the juror list. The list is provided by the court to help in determine which persons you might not like to help decide on the case. We were studying the list for the case when I said, "I think this and this and this are important."

The DA stopped, looked me in the eye, and said, "What's important is every other Friday—that's payday." I'll always remember his comment, which helps keep me grounded.

Got called for jury duty several times during my twenty-five years. While the outcome was predetermined (no defense attorney would let you on a jury), it was a day off the streets and a chance to get caught up on my reading. Day went something like this: Arrive at the jury pool room. Sign in. "Take a seat." Morning dragged on while I tried to keep awake (my normal sleep time). Go to lunch, ninety minutes long. Oh, those rough hours for the court personnel. Wait some more. Oh wow, I am with a panel of people on our way to a courtroom, yippee. We enter the sterile courtroom described earlier. All the players are sitting at their assigned seats. The defendant, his attorney, along with the county attorney all smile (trying to gain favor, hmm). We, the lemmies, dutifully march to the jury box and await the judge's introductions. The twenty-five panel members of my group now will be introduced to all the players. Not a social event—we need to be questioned if we know any of the gathered folks. Can't let any bias sneak in. Judge gives a very brief description of the events involved in this case. Many of my mates nod, akin to the little bobblehead dog you've seen in the back window of cars. I am enjoying myself, since I know where this is heading.

With all the instructions finished, the judge now asks, "Having heard my prior comments, does anyone in the panel have a problem with being able to be unbiased regarding the defendant's guilt or innocence?"

Up pops my hand. Judge says, "Yes."

I introduce myself, explaining as a police officer I know the immense difficulty involved in getting a case all the way to the court. I go on to advise while telling the truth the officer has nothing to gain; the defendant has everything to gain by telling untruths.

Judge says, "So you would be unable to render an unbiased verdict?"

"Yes, sir," I reply.

"Thank you, Officer Fribbs, for your candor. You are excused. Moving on, does anyone else have a bias to announce" (thinking he is kind of shaming me). First one then another hand goes up till the entire panel has their hands raised.

Judge asks, "Would your collective objection be similar to that stated by Officer Fribbs?"

Their bobbleheaded dog response sends all of us back to our waiting room. "Bailiff, bring up a new panel. Oh, and by the way, Officer, thanks!" I don't think he really meant thanks.

In the early years as a shift three cop, you could count on being in court most days. Usually it was city court where mostly the defendants never showed. The advantage was time spent there fell under the overtime rule, which helped the bottom line on pay day. Some years later, a Brainiac decided we should go home and wait for the court to call us if needed. Terrific—I had to essentially stay on duty till someone advised I was not needed before I could be off duty. And they didn't want to pay for this time. Enter the union and we got paid.

CHAPTER 16

Feedback

The satisfaction of helping victims and sometimes suspects was rewarding to a degree. Ten Atta boys would be wiped out by one—"Aw shit," so the saying goes. Around 1983, I was going through a divorce. I had to apply for a mortgage on the cabin I owned in Flagstaff. As luck would have it, the interest rates were around 13 percent (Jimmy Carter Days). Regular lending institutes were not interested due to poor credit, so I made an appointment with a secondary lender. I sat nervously waiting to see the loan officer of this nondescript company. The female loan officer seemed nice and was aware of my recent marital status along with a poor credit rating. We discussed the loan and my ability to pay it back. It was agreed we would meet again the next day for a decision. I wasn't having much luck with my financial goals, as the divorcee was ruining my options. I returned the next day as directed and sat across from what I hoped would be a good outcome. She looked me right in the eye and said, "I know you, but you don't remember me." Oh crap, did I arrest her some time in the past? She let me sweat a moment then handed me a victim information card. These were routinely given to victims so they would have the DR (department report) number for further reference. I read it. She never said a word. The card showed a DR number, a date, and my name. It didn't click till she referred to some parts of the incident. Like a flash, I remembered the scene.

I had been called to a family fight involving her husband and her. He was drunk, had assaulted her, and scared their daughter before leaving prior to my arrival. Her injuries were not serious, but the fight was a continuing thing with him. She said he wouldn't be back tonight, so my backup left while I took the details to make my report requesting an arrest warrant be issued for him. I had enough info for the report when she heard a vehicle cruise by she thought might be him. We walked out to the driveway as he pulled in. As he opened the door yelling and all puffed up, I took his arm and launched him face first to the concrete. "Force necessary to affect the arrest," reads the code. He was cuffed and placed in my car before you could count to ten. He had a nice goose egg on his head and was quiet after I explained how I dealt with noisy wife beater prisoners. She seemed in shock but advised she was okay as I explained her need to obtain an order of protection to keep him away. He was booked, and I went on about my business. Never went to court or heard anything about the charges, assuming a plea bargain had been reached. My loan officer was this gal. She had kept the info card after all these years, maybe five to six, and told me seeing her abusive husband knocked, hooked, and booked was the highlight of her young life.

"Do you know you are my personal hero?"

Well, no I didn't, but it was great to hear she had divorced him and she and her daughter were living a good life with a stand-up man. Yes, I got the loan at a great rate.

CHAPTER 17

Building Searches

Searching a building, a car, a house, or any other hiding place possesses its own set of dangerous issues. If you are sure a bandit is hiding, mental alert level 4 is used. Alert 3 would be for anything less. Called to the Wax Museum for an audible alarm. This building was located at the east edge of Phoenix prior to entering Tempe. One would naturally think an alarm sounding would chase away any intruder, so alert level 3 right? What if the intruder is deaf? So goes the patrol officer's mentality. Me, along with a backup, arrived to find the owner waiting. She advised the alarm was very reliable and feared someone must be inside, alert 3+. We began a systematic search of the huge building. Picture, we have wax figures in all sorts of settings to sort through while the alarm continues to ring (she forgot the code to shut it off). Everywhere I look is a potential candidate ready to spring on me. We sort through the cowboys, Indians, president, Hollywood actors, astronauts, and other famous people to clear the main room. This was nerve-wracking, thinking a smart bad guy might change clothes with one of the figures. Well, he could have! With the front displays clear, we had to go behind the scenes to search. Each display was shaped as a curved arc, thus allowing for room to walk behind the sets. Into the forbidden zone we went. Several unidentified noises had been heard, thus I had my gun out and was ready. I struggled my way through the storage boxes and other junk piled up in the area. As I came to a small clearing out of the corner of my eye above me, I saw a figure to my left towering over me. Swinging my pistol, I dropped to one knee and started to put a trigger pull on the gun, sighting my target. It was Jesus way up on the cross. Yes, I almost had plugged a wax figure of our Savior. I would have never lived that down. The search turned up nothing but a good story for the ages.

An alert level 4 search took place one night at a Mom and Pop grocery store across from the Duppa Villa housing projects. The projects were subsidized housing for low/no income families. Upon arrival, we found a ladder to the roof in the alley behind the store. Further investigation revealed a swamp cooler on the roof pushed over. That would provide access to the store. The building was surrounded, and a K-9 unit was called for. Watching through the windows inside, I saw one of the robbers walking around. Bingo. This was level 4+. Shortly, the dog handler, Officer Bill S., and his "Land Shark German Shepherd Chinook" arrived. You saw the movie *Jaws*? now you are getting the picture as this dog was getting worked up by Bill. A word about the police dogs. They were trained to bite movement, resistance, and the smell of fear. Side note—the dog handlers always say, "Oh no! Our dogs are friendly except when working." Bullshit to that; these cousins to alligators wanted to rip your face off—period. Since I had been involved in two or three incidents prior with them, I gave these carnivores a wide berth. The market owner who had provided us with keys was also told to stay clear.

Bill opened the door and announced, "Phoenix Police. I have a dog who wants to come in and bite your balls off. This is your only warning to come out before I turn him lose!" The dog was about to flip out, barking his head off as Officer Bill restrained him. Later, the suspects, who spoke no "Englass," told us all they heard of Bill's announcement was "Blah blah blah blah, etc." Having received no response from inside, Bill turned Schnook loose to search. In short order, screaming was heard as the canine had found his first meal. First one down—how did we know there were more? They (bandits) never worked alone. One down and one to go. The first guy had received a few bites to his hands before giving up. Now on to numero 2. He was hiding up on a shelf where the dog couldn't get to him but gave up anyway. Bill had him handcuffed and was leading him out the front door when the fool kicked at the dog. Picture a shark-feeding frenzy as "Jaws" went after his knee. It took a moment to stop him from feeding. Blood was squirting everywhere as Stupid withered in agony. Fire rescue was on the scene and went to work, trying to stop the bleeding. We rushed him to County Hospital as he was bleeding out. In the treatment room, I watched as the doc pushed a huge hypo needle with benzidine into the holes left by the canine's teeth only to see it leak out other holes. I saw twelve to fifteen holes leaking.

They finally stopped the flow while the Doc announced, "You will most likely lose that leg to infection."

"I fought the law and the law won!" God, I so loved the job.

On one dark and quiet night, me and the Pear responded to a silent alarm call at a small standalone office building. The rear door appeared to have been jimmied with fresh marks on it. We entered, and being seasoned officers, instead of roaming around with flashlights, we turned on all the lights. Pretty smart, huh? I entered the hallway with my trusty pistol ready. At the end of the hall, out of the corner of my eye, I saw a figure emerging who had a gun; he ducked back when I did. I told this robber to come out with his hands held high. No response. Again I boomed at him, "Get your hands up and show yourself." Still no response! *Okay, you asked for it*, was my thought as I swung around the corner, gun ready to find me facing me in the mirror at the end of the hall. Yep … We finished the search and were waiting for the owner to arrive, kinda laughing at my near shootout.

"Can I come out now?" came a shaky voice from under a desk. Holy crap! A bandit had been hiding in a space under one of the desks the whole time. He was quickly scooped up. Needless to say, these two old veterans learned a lesson that day about searching.

An officer told the story of his recruit on her academy training ride. Silent alarm response brought them to a large warehouse. No signs of forced entry, so after getting keys, they entered. They had just begun searching when the rookie turned and ran out of the building. Her training officer went in search of her.

"What happened?" he asked.

"In the academy, we were taught if we heard a noise we didn't recognize, we should run for cover." Really? She had heard the time clock make a tick-tock. Granted, it was a noise most wouldn't recognize, but what about leaving your partner alone? And the beat goes on.

CHAPTER 18

Incompetence in the Ranks

It sometimes is hard to believe some of the officers I worked with went through the same training I did. In watching them do their duties, I wondered how much confusion and maybe real fear ran undercurrent for them. Radio advised District 7 (our northern boundary) had a police unit being followed by an unknown vehicle for an unknown reason. Huh! Pull over and confront the follower—what the hell is going on? We switched to their channel and monitored. The officer's voice was nearing panic as he described his efforts to lose the tail. He was in a marked unit; what could possibly be going on? "The chase" was heading into our area, so we were off to investigate. I spotted the cars racing south down Twenty-Fourth Street from Roosevelt. Police car in front, bad guy right behind him. I swung my car in front of the bandit, cutting him off as I forced it to the curb. The "deer caught in the headlights" look of the driver told me he wasn't expecting this. I charged the driver's door to find a young man, his young wife, and a very small baby in the car.

The officer who had started this remained in his car some one hundred feet away. What the hell was going on!

The driver told me they were trying to get to County Hospital with their sick baby. Only knowing the general direction to the hospital, he had flagged the officer, now in question, down to get directions. The officer told him to follow him to the hospital. Their baby was sick, but we weren't dealing with an emergency here. I went to the officer still sitting in his car to question the event. A puzzled look came over his face as I related what I had been told. Silence followed his puzzled look, then he said, "Oh yeah, I did say that." OMG! We pointed the couple to the hospital, whose twelve-story building was across the street. They drove off with me shaking my head.

While I was still a POW in 700 district, I was assigned to evaluate a probationary officer that was reported to be shaky at best. "Take a look at him and see if we should keep him." Terrific! He was riding solo so he had nearly a year on. Seemed like a bright enough fellow; will call him Barney for reasons that should be obvious. Small stature with soft little hands. Intelligent though. I followed him around on calls till an accident involving a drunk driver running into a house came out for any unit to respond. I answered up for him to respond. The scene was quite chaotic, with firemen, neighbors, and the homeowner holding on to the drunk driver. Barney just stood there, surveying the scene like a spectator. "Cuff him and put him in your car," I said twice. Very reluctantly, he moved to complete this task. I pushed him forward and helped put on the silver bracelets on the belligerent. I next had to tell Barney, "Put him in your car now." The homeowner was now in my ear, wanting to know what was going to be done about the house damage. I got him away from our arrest and tried to take in the scene. The prisoner was in Barney's car, but I could see a light coming for the compartment he was held in. I went to that location to discover the turd had slipped his cuffs and was lighting matches. What had Barney been doing all this time? He had become a spectator from outside the car. Yes, I went ape shit. Holy cow, this was worse than I could ever imagine. I had radio assign another unit to take over the scene as Barney and I processed the drunk. We went to the 800 district station to accomplish this. I told him I would help, but the detail was his to work through. OMG, on nearly twelve months and didn't know how to process a DUI. Who had trained or checked on this guy's progress? The drunk in the holding cell was making all kinds of demands and being a real butthole. The other officers in the station were shaking their heads in disbelief that Barney wasn't controlling him. I finally lost it and went in the cell to bring the loudmouth out for processing. He had pissed and spit all over the floor, which caused me to lose my balance when I grabbed him. I went down to one knee, about to lose control, when I called for Barney to grab him. To my disbelief, no Barney. He was frozen in the doorway, unable to move. An officer, hearing the commotion, pushed him aside rushed in and helped me regain control. We thumped the drunk a little to ensure he knew who was in charge. The added officer agreed to assist me in processing the 390 (drunk), and I told Barney to go back out to the street and wait for me to contact him. "Don't advise radio you are available."

The drunk, now understanding that real police officers, were present caused no further problems and did as he was told.

Drunk Driver turned in front of me during a pursuit
Estimated collision speed 72 mph
Note door frame and window damage passenger side
resulting from attempts by PD officers to extricate
my partner. Then note my door is totally open?

It took some time to get him ready for transport to jail, and about an hour passed before I was ready to head back out to the street. Having finished with the drunk and regaining my composure, I set up a 10-25 (meet) with Barney. He was completely defeated. I asked him about his conduct, lack of knowledge, and courage. He admitted to freezing up at the station, stating he hadn't been in any kind of physical confrontation on the street. I explained that not everyone was cut out to be a police officer and there was no shame in that. He told me he had joined the PD hoping to make a man of himself and now knew that wasn't going to happen. I agreed to allow him to approach our supervisor to resign prior to my reporting the incident. He was gone by the end of the shift. Kinda felt sorry for him till I noticed my beautifully spit-shined boots had been scuffed in the tussle.

We had a new rookie transfer into our District. He was reported to have been an Officer for a Department from out of state. He was big enough, but new people always bear watching. I heard him go Code 6 (traffic stop) and made his backup. He was running a records check on his radio as I pulled up. The subject was cooperative while we waited for the wants/warrants check. Radio said, "10-12/907/10-52." Translation—"Stand by, a backup is on its way. Your subject has a warrant." Oh, those codes.

He advised radio, "Code 4," and went to put the driver in his patrol car as I secured the guy's car. I asked if he had searched the subject before putting him in the back seat. I was concerned since he had stowed him so quickly. He said he did and left with the prisoner for the station. I went back in service.

A few minutes later, Radio asked me to go to the station to do a Breathalyzer test. At the station, while I was preparing the machine for the BA test, I heard a knock on a holding room door. Investigating, I found the prior mentioned prisoner inside the room holding a pistol pointed down. "Do you want this?" he asked. I took the gun and went in search of the rookie. He didn't seem all that surprised as I read him the riot act. Had this type of thing happened to him before? I wondered. I did report the incident to his supervisor for training purposes. The gun had been in his prisoner's boot when the officer did his sloppy search. Police history books are full of dead cops from sloppy searches. A few weeks later, I was making a backup for this same cop on a family fight. The wife claimed her husband had punched her as attested to her bruised eye. She thought he was hiding outside. Didn't think he had any weapons. We went in search of this now number 1(to be arrested). I heard a struggle in a corner of the backyard, which sounded as if my partner had found him. I ran that direction to confront the suspect, now armed with a big black metal night stick.

Gee, that looks like the kind officer's carry. He charged me raising the pole over his head as my pistol came out of my holster. I was pulling on my trigger as I saw the baton fly away after striking my upraised forearm. The weapon's threat now gone, I reholstered my gun and took the assaulter to the ground. Would require a run to County Hospital before being allowed to book this guy.

Yep, it was the officer's stick that the suspect had taken from the other officer.

Thought about charging our fouling up officer with aiding and abetting for suppling the weapon. He soon left the district.

CHAPTER 19

Morbid Curiosity

The scene of major auto accidents seems to hold a morbid fascination to people. Often, we had to delegate an officer just to keep people out of our scene. First responders know their way around the carnage while snoopers can get run over while trying to get a peek. Maybe the flare's bright light or the smoke from it caused folks to ask and do strange things. A major accident usually relegated you to a minor role once the detail detectives arrived. Did I mention bored cops equal trouble? Flare pattern's guiding traffic around the scene left little to do. Some citizen/officer exchanges at wreck scenes.

"Officer, I live down there."

"Congratulations."

"I need to go that way to get home."

"Well, ma'am, I would let you but it would require you driving over the dead bodies and wreckage down there" or "Just follow the flares."

"What flares?" Speaking of flares, I kept a few in my sap pocket (sewn in pocket on the pants leg for leather covered device used sometimes for attitude adjustments) for replacing burnt-up flares. Or for easy access to launch one at some fool that's just driven through your pattern.

What was needed to stop them driving through your "road is closed" pattern was a flare thirty, forty, fifty feet long (whatever your street size was). Usually they avoided driving on top of the glowing stick.

"Officer, was anyone hurt?" as they were looking at the mangled wreckage, first responders, ambulance crew all working feverishly to extricate a subject.

"No, we're just conducting some training on a live subject, ma'am."

I am reminded of the tale of an LA cop on the scene of a major accident, who had become tired of the gawkers, responded to a lady driving by question, "Was anyone hurt, Officer?"

He reached inside the overturned car, lifted the severed head, and said, "Well, this one got bounced around a little bit."

True story? I wouldn't doubt it. As if by magic when the bodies were taken to the hospital or morgue the crowd disappeared. Accidents were, in a way, small crime scenes. They contained all the elements of a criminal incident. Victims, suspects, witness, liars, and confusion it was all there. We would arrive, separate the player while collecting driver license, insurance, and registration info as we made the necessary calls for wreckers. If the accident didn't have serious injuries or a driver who had left the scene, we started by questioning witnesses not involved in the incident. While they often were confused, they had no axe to grind and tried to provide accurate info. Eyewitness's confusion had been explained: they hear or see a collision a millisecond after it occurs, then their brain fast-forwards to place the vision prior to the event. I had people get mad at me when I proved to them they were completely wrong about what they saw. Of course you needed to know this for an accurate investigation. Their statements, after the smoke had cleared, were usually accurate for such as who was driving which car, if the subject had run, etc. Our job was to investigate, clear the intersection or street, issue citations, and draw a diagram to file with the report. These accidents varied in intensity from fender benders with a couple of tickets issued to major follow-ups at hospitals. During day shift, you could usually get a motorcycle officer to take the wreck cause it was hot out, and that would get them into a cooler place to do their report. Worked for them.

CHAPTER 20

Choir Practice

We worked hard and played even harder. There was often a need to debrief after a wild Friday or Saturday night. The method and means was some beer and a trip to Policeman's Park after shift. It was located away from the station and in an area being bulldozed for the airport expansion, in other words around and near nothing. The squad needed to vent and relax after the pressure of the often violent game played out on the streets. Years later, crisis intervention groups were invented to due debriefings. (Don't think they brought beer though.)

However, these crisis units only responded to major incidents. Our nightly crises were accumulative, so we had to take care of ourselves. Thinking back, maybe there should have been a happy medium drawn between beer parties and venting. Anyway, it worked for us. Ill feelings were worked out, and general resentments were cleared up. An example might be a trooper thinking someone had ducked a call that turned out to be a lot of work for them. With discussion, it usually was found out no one had ducked the call; they were tied up with their own problem call. If it was discovered they were guilty, their shame was exposed and warned to not happen again. So it went, most often we all went home with issues cleared up. You might wonder why this was important. Your very life often depended on the officers you worked with, and no one could afford to have an ill feeling about them. Choir practice, as it was known came to an abrupt end, one night under the better known as Seventh Avenue Bridge,

Seemed a squad would meet there to debrief and got carried away when they found a drunk invading their private grounds. While the true story will never be known the drunk after being escorted away called the on-duty police and complaints were filed. We were under the leadership of Ruben O. He was a piece of work. He had risen through the ranks without much street time and was very quick to jump to the conclusion that his street cops were worthless necessities. When a complaint was presented to him, he seemed to believe the whiners. The short of it—he fired the seven officers. Later, investigation questioned the haste in which it was conducted. Normally, suspension would precede firing. Almost overnight, they were gone. The troops, two sergeants, and five officers were thankful that we had a strong union that went to the wall with them.

Some two years later, after several ranking officers' recounting of events involving the decision to fire was questioned before the civil service board and other investigating agencies, the seven were exonerated and given back their jobs. The city paid large sums of money to them for the wrong but they were never the same having had their spirits broken. It did stop choir practice all together. Officers were told if they were somewhere and knew someone present had drank too much that officer could be held responsible for the other persons actions. We will never know what effect this had on officers not being able to defuse the old way. The job went on, and we continued to work in spite of our lack of leadership.

Our squad sergeant Steve S. was promoted to lieutenant and left the district. He was replaced by a series of new sergeants. None stayed very long, as I suspect they were afraid of being responsible for our style of police work. The beat went on.

CHAPTER 21

New Sergeants for 52 Bravo

Sergeant Bob W. got the squad after Sergeant Steve left. Bob W., having ridden a desk came from downtown and wasn't ready for the streets. Nice guy but way out of his element. He did try very hard to emulate our former leader's style and actually got pretty good before he transferred away. One incident in which Jimmy may or may not have slammed the door leaving a courtroom brought Sergeant Bob W. to a boil. We had a city court judge who was routinely dismissing our parking tickets without hearings. Basically opened court by advising anyone there for parking tickets to see his bailiff for dismissal. After one hearing when he did this, Jimmy left the room in a huff, thus the door slamming incident. After Sergeant Bob got a complaint from the court, he called us into his office and thought he was going to rake us over the coals. He began his tirade by getting all red in the face with the veins sticking way out in his neck. He went on for a while till he could tell we weren't impressed. He, of course, hadn't asked for our side of the story, so we weren't caring about his performance. He finally stopped and took a breath. He was really pissed, and we didn't care and he knew it.

As he paused, Jimmy said, "Any interest in knowing what really happened, Sergeant?"

Sergeant Bob's face showed the shock of someone realizing they had goofed. It was explained the door hinges were broken, causing it to swing wide, hitting the jam. The judge (later committed to Arizona State Mental Hospital) and his paranoia, along with being a nutcase, had taken it to mean we were disrespectful. Our broken spring story was all bullshit, of course, but once again, I had pulled the Pear out of the fire with my command of the English language. Following Sergeant Bob's little tirade, he had calmed down and wanted to have a heart-to-heart chat now. He asked about the squad's morale and generally beat around the bush about police work. He finally got to the point and asked, "How do you rate me as a supervisor down here in this action filled district?"

I knew, as it was coming out of his mouth, he had made a very big mistake to ask such a question. Jimmy's reply was, "We think you are a spineless jellyfish."

The silence was complete. Bob W. turned to me, looking for help. My only comment was yep. We left the office having cleared the air and watched Sergeant Bob W. steadily improve as a supervisor in our district. He must have found his spine as he even surprised himself with some of his calls on the street. We were kicking ass again, and complaints were rolling off his back. He truly was enjoying being a sergeant. The winds of change were blowing for police work.

CHAPTER 22

The New Breed of Supervisor

New supervisors were being taught to distrust their officers. They were to catch their troops goofing off. The cops were not to be trusted was the word. If a new sergeant didn't catch his people short, he was considered non-sergeant material. This attitude came all the way down from the top. Our chief and several assistant chiefs were less than admired by the troops who knew of their performance when they worked on the streets. This new breed of supervisor was underhanded and not men to be trusted. Several had showed this during the Seventh Avenue seven hearings. It was a difficult time as you were constantly second-guessed. An example would help to explain this. Jimmy and I were riding a two-man car one night and decided to become a walking beat. It was relatively slow, so we went out on foot near the Mexican bar, the Calderon.

Next door was a smaller bar, and we noticed a patron standing out front on the sidewalk drinking a beer. This of course was forbidden. He was watching for a squad car and was quite surprised when I walked up alongside him and told him about going to jail for that kind of behavior. What I said was, "Do you want a trip to jail, stupid?" He knew what I meant and grudgingly walked back inside the bar. We appeared to walk away and waited just out of sight. *Poof*, like magic, dip shit walks right back out and assumes his original position. A sip of his beer, and my nightstick sent his can flying. We spun him around, he tried to resist, and my arm around his neck, we went to the ground. He wouldn't bring his arms around for handcuffing, so Jimmy began punching his shoulder to make him loosen his arm. That worked, and as I was putting cuffs on him, I noticed new Sergeant Joe W. (not be confused with our Sergeant W) watching the struggle from a safe distance. We completed the arrest putting the guy in our car. I walked over to Sergeant Joe and asked him if he was just an observer tonight or was he working, referring to his lack of participation during the arrest. He said, "I am sorry, but I am going to write you guys up for excessive force." I was floored. What the hell was he talking about? This was a simple takedown. He claimed that Jimmy had punched the guy after he was cuffed. This was that new breed of sergeant I was talking about. Well, Jimmy hadn't punched him after the cuffs were on, and I blew up.

Sergeant Joe W. said, "I saw what I saw" and left. I heard him ask radio for the lieutenant's location, and I told radio we would also like to see the lieutenant after we booked our prisoner. I did this to let Sergeant Joe know he wasn't going to get away with his "make-believe" story. We booked the suspect with no problems and came back out to the street to hear Sergeant Joe. and Lieutenant Mike F. checking out at the jail. We went back to work, and soon Lieutenant Mike. called to set up a meet. He wanted to know our version of the story. Mike was a good officer and sergeant, but as a new lieutenant, he seemed a little shaky. First, I told him there wasn't two versions, only the truth, which was ours. I began recounting the incident when he tried to stop me, saying he would have to write me up if I said I had grabbed the suspect's neck.

"Write away," was my reply. "If you want the true story, listen." We made sure he understood the guy wasn't punched after the cuffs were on. I was really pissed at this new breed of supervisor and almost lost it when he told me the next part of the saga. He and Sergeant Joe W. had gone to the jail to try to solicit a complaint from our prisoner. I was seeing red. The prisoner had told them to go to hell, as it was he who had acted stupid after the officer had warned him. Imagine this! I was livid! I told Lieutenant Mike, daring him to write this up, he would be the laughing stock of the district. I reminded Lieutenant Mike, to remember, we do police work on the streets. The incident went away, but Sergeant Joe W never forgot it, I know. Years later, when Sergeant Joe W. became a lieutenant, he tried unsuccessfully to bring Jimmy W. and me down. This is just one example of how the department was changing. We were actually told to stop subduing people using the chokehold. This hold, which cuts off the oxygen to the brain, had been the main way to subdue violent offenders forever. The departments didn't offer an alternative to use other than hitting them with a nightstick or fist. Now I asked you which was going to do the most damage to the suspect.

One morning, as I was coming off shift, a day guy asked for someone to do a Breathalyzer test on his prisoner. I was the only tester available, so off I went. The prisoner wasn't cooperating and became combative, so rather than throw a choke on him, I just slugged him right in the chops, splitting both his lips. Now since a simple control hold wasn't available, this guy was off to the hospital for repairs. It wasn't making sense anymore. Mind you, the criminal element hadn't been told we weren't to use the old methods so they still resisted arrest the same old ways. The times were very difficult for us Old Warriors. The department continued on its campaign to wanting less and less physical contact. "The job just gets easier and easier" was the new motto. For the new people, who were being taught in the academy, the new methods would work, but it grated on the old-timers, who could see the handwriting on the wall. It was time to come off "Zero Dark Thirty" (shift three) and go to days.

CHAPTER 23

Coming in from the Dark

It was with great reluctance and relief to some supervisors I submitted my transfer request. Days would require a somewhat modified approach to my police activities. I had been working the streets around ten years now and was going through a divorce. I was drinking too much but never on the job. Rule one, never do anything on the job that would cost you money (suspension days) or your job. A new work schedule was to be four days at ten hours instead of the old five/eights. The entire police department's patrol division was reorganizing its districts and squads. All personnel were to rebid for the shift and squad they wanted. It was to be done by seniority. When the process shook out, I had to give up the day slot I wanted to allow Jimmy W. to get day shift. This required me to work for one of day shift's biggest dip shits. He was black and carried a big chip on his shoulder. Years earlier, as an officer, his performance at the scene on a small riot involving blacks had been questioned. Officer Jim T. had his head split open by a thrown rock. Other officers reported my new sergeant-to-be failed to react before or afterward. There were a lot of angry officers at that incident, but nothing came of his ineptness. Now he was a sergeant who would supervisor me? Right. This situation was only temporary, so I was okay with it.

The first day working for him, he called me into his office and complained about my mustache. He admitted it was within regulation, but he didn't like it. I just stared at him, letting him know what a complete Adam Henry (police talk for asshole) I knew he was. I knew it was going to be a long shift. I stayed away from him as much as possible and daily told Jimmy W. how much he owed me.

Soon enough, I made my way to Sergeant Larry O's squad and began having fun again. This squad had Jimmy, me, Mike B., Jerry H., and Al G., among others. We served many a search warrant. This proved embarrassing to the detectives. Jerry H. had a nose for finding stolen property and knew how to draw up a search warrant. We found ourselves in neighboring city on a regular basis. Sergeant O, a fine supervisor, said, "Go where it takes you."

I was quite happy working 900 District but always wanted to be a counselor at the academy. I guess my lousy experience at the academy as a recruit had tainted me to a degree. I wanted to right this wrong and got my chance in August of 1980. I was told to report to the academy on a Thursday for a class starting on Monday. I was ready physically and mentally but a little unsure of my duties. I met with Sergeant Jim M. (Tempe PD supervisor), my new boss. He said if I was unsure of any of the recruits' questions, advise them, "I'll get back to you." That was simple, huh?

CHAPTER 24

Return to the Streets

Following my stint at the academy, I went back to the streets and more exciting days. I will cover some highlights. The following are in no particular order, just some famous or infamous events.

It was 900 District, with its usual assortment of whore, dopers, dealers, pimps, transvestites, and other social misfits on most every corner. Jimmy and I were a good team, having learned each other's moves down to a tee. A head or arm movement, a voice inflection, a certain way of standing—it all meant something to the other partner. A look from either one might mean "Circle behind this douche bag, he's going down." It was a beautiful thing. We almost always struck first. This may seem harsh to the unschooled, but it worked to keep us from injury and minimized the damage to the perp.

A typical Friday to Saturday night would yield about six to ten arrests for the squad both nights. Drunkenness was almost always at the root. DUI, disorderly conduct, domestic issues—they all had the abuse of alcohol in them. I don't recall ever going to a family fight wherein the parties weren't drunk or drinking. Sober people just aren't a big part of law enforcement's daily activities.

The job becomes a *Punta* (Mexican for "whore"); you find missing work that is just not thought of. You might've missed a big shittery when you were on your days off; that just couldn't happen. It would be like an athlete training for the big game and being benched. No amount of words can really describe it. We took down parties large and small the same way. When it had been determined a party wasn't breaking up on its own, usually we would select the loudest mouth and/or the biggest guy, and down they went hard. This was fire for effect. Usually one or two others would make an attempt to interfere with the arrest, and they went also. The crowd was given the following advice: "Anyone else want to go with them?" This would begin the somewhat orderly process of the party dispersing. We did not take bullshit from people—period; it didn't happen. On occasion, we would have a new squad member transfer in. They had a very short period to become used to our ways or they found another squad to work for. The reputation of the squad was such that most shied away before considering working with us.

While Sergeant Steve S. was our supervisor, we were left alone by most of the brass. If they did have a problem with our methods, Sarge shielded us. His primary concern was keeping the guys lean and mean. If that meant hiding the complaints and concerns from the guys, well, okay. Sergeant theorized telling the troops would only take the fire out of them, and that wasn't to happen. We couldn't have had the reign we did without several things being in place. The districts were run by a captain who was left alone because downtown didn't micromanage as they did later.

District Captain/General

A district captain was like a war general. His word was law, and all obeyed. An example will explain. Call came in of a 962 (injury accident) on Twenty-Fourth Street East Van Buren. I arrived to find a VW into a light pole. Lone occupant a very drunk driver, minor damage to the car and pole. The driver went about 380 lbs. and barely was able to get out of the bug. Officer Jim K wanted the call to help his training for going to motors.

"All yours," was my response and I went 10-8 (back in service). Ten to fifteen minutes later, radio cleared Sergeant S. to head to the station for a 901H there. 901H—dead body? I had been on about three years with reserve time and knew what a 901H was, but I still looked it up on my radio code sheet.

I telephoned the station, and Officer Frank D. answered, telling me, "The fucking guy is dead, man!" He was referring to the drunk from the VW. Not needing to be told, I headed for the station. I walked in the front door, noticing the paramedics sitting on a table. VW man was lying on the floor with a chalk line drawn around him. The quiet in the room was deafening. Sergeant S. was in a far corner on the phone. I was listening to Jim K. explain how he and Frank had tried to drag the drunk out of the holding cell to do the Breathalyzer test. He was too heavy for only two of them to move, so while they pondered this, he just stopped breathing. The guy just stopped breathing after moaning and slobbering on himself. Fire had been called, and they found no pulse, so they were awaiting our decision.

Sergeant S. hung up the phone and said, "Take him to County Hospital. Captain says he isn't dead—he can only die at the hospital."

Everyone picked a body part and carted him to the ambulance. John H. (alias) died at the Maricopa County Medical Center, a.k.a. County Hospital. His combined intoxication level (drugs and alcohol) was .56 percent. Doctors said that was a lethal dose.

A little later, when the detectives and internal affairs got to the station, they were pissed. Sergeants, lieutenants, captains, and majors were everywhere. Heads were going to roll. Who moved the body? There was a cover-up, etc. The finger-pointing was incredible. Remember, a very drunk man had accidentally committed suicide by abusing himself to the point of causing his own death. After the smoke had cleared, Captain G. reminded the assembled sleuths the man died at County Hospital—go check the records.

We were quietly reminded when a drunk was that far out of it, maybe a better place for them would be the hospital, not the station. The lesson learned: "No one dies in the police station."

Maricopa County Medical Center
AKA County Hospital

CHAPTER 25

Airport Detail, Here I Come

Working days was a very different world. You could see everything. The flashlight, that extension of your arm, was put away. People waved to you with their whole hand, not just one finger, as you went by; little kids came up to your car to ask for swim tickets for the public pool. The businesses were open, and life was revolving everywhere around you. I didn't like it one bit. I didn't know any of the criminals on the street. It was in my eighteenth year when Sergeant Jerry B. took me under his wing. He gave me his Dutch Uncle talk about settling down and going with the flow. I think my attitude was "We're the cops and they're not," meaning we were right and criminals weren't. My problem came when there weren't criminals everywhere like night shift. I started to take a slower approach to contacts. I might take the time to have a cup of coffee with a victim at their home. When advice was requested, I look time to thoroughly answer questions. On night shift, there just wasn't time to slowly act. I was slowly getting along with days. The Action Jackson in me was dissolving. Sergeant B transferred to the airport unit, and I worked for several nondescript new sergeants. It was time for a major change for me.

Sergeant B. had been at the airport about six months when he called me to meet him at the airport one morning. We had coffee in Terminal 2. My absence from the street had been cleared with my sergeant, so we talked about old times as an hour passed. He pointed to his handheld police radio and said, "Notice not one call has come across it?" Unheard of on the streets, even on day shift. He said "Now don't you think it's about time you get out of the streets and take things a lot easier?"

I was speechless. Leave the rush of the street? It's all I had known for eighteen years. He went on to explain the airport detail, while in full uniform, wasn't like the mean streets. A much more friendly conduct was exercised at the airport. Our job was more toward helping and making people feel safe. Oh, by the way, I would just about double my salary due to the overtime available. I began, for the first time in my career, thinking about what my retirement money would look like. Retirement pay was based on our gross wages, thus more pay meant more money in retirement. Now I ain't no math wizard, but this was making good sense. I had two years to go to complete my twenty years, which would yield me 50 percent of my pay for life. Or I could stay till twenty-five years and get 62 ½ percent. With the overtime at the airport, I was looking at nearly doubling my pension by making this transfer. I'll admit I was unsure about leaving the rough-and-tumble world I had grown so used to. Jimmy and I talked it over, and we put in our papers and were soon the airport detail's newest plebes. This New World couldn't have been any different if we had been transported to another planet. The detail's equipment was all new, with no shortages. Overtime, a nonexistent thing on the street, was yours for the asking. Double shifts, working your days off, airport construction projects—all were time and half pay, all of which would reflect on increasing your pension. I couldn't believe what was happening.

The airport detail was paid by the airport budget, thus the city didn't care how much we were making. It sure pissed off many downtown police supervisors to see airport cops making lots more money than them. We often worked eighty hours a week, so family time was very limited. The goal was to build up my pension. The required change was gradual and took some adjustment on my part. Still, some good times were had during the seven years I worked there.

I had arrived still full of the street mentality (take no bullshit), which caused some early issues. Radio reported a loudmouth drunk in terminal 2. Bobby W. and I went to investigate finding just that. Big Good Ole Boy, drunk and obnoxious while threatening anyone who looked at him. This wasn't going to happen on my watch. I heard enough to make a disorderly conduct charge, walked up to him, and told him to shut up and leave the building.

"Is that right, Hoss?" was his reply just before I swept his feet out. He crashed to the floor with me on top. He was roped and hogtied in eight seconds flat. The amassed crowd of traveling folks broke out in applause. That was a different reaction, but I enjoyed it. Loudmouth was now in a holding cell crying like a baby. I booked him, knowing he would be released about twelve hours later. Sober, he could continue on his journey to a friend's funeral out of state. Paying customers didn't like being told *no*. I did receive a citizen complaint, when a flying passenger, who was upset about his connections, had to be quieted down. Actually, our contact went something like this …

"Point your finger at me, raise your voice, and you will spend the night in jail, slick. I'm the cops and not the airlines." My mentor, Sergeant Jerry B., sat me down and suggested I remember the airport was different than the streets he and I had grown up on. We discussed the traveling public carrying of video cameras and how some people only see what they want at the scene of an incident. In short, "Pull in your horns, Cowboy."

I agreed. We got a call of a female out of control in the Southwest Terminal. *Crap, here we go again.* Officer Dave R. was my backup and asked me if I would let him handle the call. *Sure, I guess*, was my thought. We could hear her yelling from some distance away as we approached. A crowd had formed, but I was determined to follow Sgt. Jerry B's advice and backed away as Dave took the lead. She was drunk and demanding. He listened to her tirade, and suddenly they sat down and seemed to be having a cordial conversation. Dave gave me a Code 4, so I left still pissed at this disturbance of the peace. Moral here—there is more than one way to handle things. Dave later told me he reminded her as a grandmother, she wouldn't want her kiddies to see her acting that way, huh?

Events and a calmness began to come together, and I actually got used to doing mostly nothing. An occasional irate customer had to be contacted (I later learned the airlines, with their "too bad, so sad" attitude, caused most of their own problems).

The days on the airport detail were mostly filled with answering question of the traveling public.

My specialty was watching for elderly folks that appeared to be lost or confused. Remember, even seemingly alert and orientated people can wander around "America's Mazes," a.k.a., airport. The idea a family would bring an elderly member to a big-city airport and drop them off to fend for themselves blew my mind.

Event went something like this:

"Howdy, ma'am/sir, are you flying out with us today?"

"Yes, I think so."

"Which airlines for you?"

"Well, I'm not rightly sure."

OMG. I do not lie. Usually they knew what city was their destination, so we had a starting point. It was like solving a little mystery. One clue lead to another, concluding with me introducing them to the flight crew. Often the flight crew/attendants would take over, putting them on board early. Not really *police* work, you say? "To Protect and Serve," reads the motto. All I needed was a cape to complete my "officer to the rescue" outfit.

Clear of my rescue mission, I would hang around the information counter, not looking at the mostly beautiful ladies passing by. I will share some airport questions asked.

"Officer, where are the B gates?"

Looking to my side, I would point. "Be right over there." Of course, the Giant B might have been a big hint.

"Officer?"

"Yes."

"I see those elevators over there go up. Where are the down ones?" I do not lie. I think maybe the escalators caused their confusion. Usually, I would direct them to the bank of elevators on the other side. Nothing to be gained by explaining Mr. Otis designed them to go up and down.

It was so refreshing to talk to folks whose intelligence was equal to your own. Having spent the last years listening to conversation that started off with "Shit man motherfucker," etc., my new customers were refreshing to my ears. Sometimes on EVB, the combined IQ of a group might approach only double digits. Of course that made dealing with them quite simple. The level of stupidity sometimes got so bad in order to clear your mind, we would go visit the two place where mostly intelligent people were found, our hospitals.

"How long will it take me to get to my gate?" was always an interesting question since I didn't have the foggiest idea which gate. I may have on occasion pointed to the last person in a block-long line near the check point, stating they might know. A lady one day pointed out George Burns walking through the terminal smoking a big fat stogie. I guess she wanted me to enforce the "No smoking in the building" rule. Well, knowing Burns's reputation for being a grumpy old man I declined. She was aghast. What did she expect? He didn't know about the "No smoking" rule so he would apologize? Yeah, when pigs fly. Most likely he'd tell me to kiss his ninety-nine-year-old ass, and what was I going to do about it? I think she wanted cuffs on this old, old American icon. Wouldn't be happening by this old street cop. Oh, sure, she filed a complaint, and the beat goes on.

Wayward Husband

I guess all major city airports security details are run the same way as Sky Harbor was.

The details consisted of a lieutenant, several sergeants, and squads of officers.

Our security detail's existence was to serve the airport's needs. Everything requiring police presence happening in a small town could and would happen in our little domain.

Remember, highly stressed alcohol-infused people make up a great deal of the travelers. We will tattle on a few of them. "Contact female near gate B-2 reference family issues. While there, also contact bartender nearby to remove unwanted guest." Could it be related? I walked into the bar near B-2 checkpoint, expecting to find both problems. Bingo. A very attractive young female stood out as she waved to me. She was sitting at one of those little round tables they use to ensure you don't get too comfortable. Her eyes were swollen and teary, leaving her with a somewhat disheveled look. At the table with her was another female. I approached and ask how could I help. "That's the son of a bitch [pointing at a business-dressed man sitting on a stool at the bar] I'm married to sitting there with his whore!"

Didn't see that coming. That was one of the clearest answers I had ever received in my time on the job. I said, "Now in our normal speaking voice, what can I help you with?"

Her outburst over, she explained she and her girlfriend had followed her two-timer husband to the airport today. He was to have been off on a business trip. Instead she found him in the bar with his new main squeeze. Both were sporting boarding passes for the same flight, imagine that.

Of course, the call of the unwanted guest was her, whom I was thinking had created quite a scene prior to my arrival. She was spent by now, readily agreeing to leave. The issue at hand, while very intense to all, wasn't per se a police problem. She was holding her composure pretty well as we exited the gate area. "Officer, would you do me one favor before I leave?"

"No, ma'am, I can't kill your cheating, no-good slime ball husband," was what I expected to say.

Her request was I talk with the transgressor's mother on the phone about the incident. Very unusual request indeed. Jilted lady explained his mother wouldn't believe her about the incident. Sure, why not, who better to learn about your scum-sucking, unfaithful son than a Phoenix police officer, right? Yep, I knew I could expect to get discipline if he bitched to management about me. Weighing the pros and cons, Lady won out. I did take the phone and explain who I was and what part I had played in this made-for-TV drama soap opera. I overheard Lady say, "Now let's see him try to lie his way out of this to his Mommy Dearest."

Security Checkpoints

Of all the reasons for the police presence at the airport's number one is responding to the checkpoints for weapon finds. "Aw," you scoff, "really? Bring a weapon through a checkpoint?"

Six times I responded to the call with one being invisible.

A busy Saturday morning was interrupted by our emergency tone of a weapon found at Checkpoint C. I arrived within the required three-minute response time as required by the Federal Aviation Administration (FAA). I was directed to one of the x-ray machines and saw the image on its screen, of two pistols in a backpack. "Okay, bring them out," was my command. *Whirl, whirl,* the machine sounded as nothing emerged from inside it. "Okay, bring it out," I shouted. Nothing. I leaned over far enough to look inside to see a very large void. It was empty—nada. "Where is the bag, and better yet, where is the owner?" was my next request. The lack of any person around was my first clue. The bag, owner, and contents were gone. The screener, maybe at the sight of the gun, had fled. The supervisor was present but didn't have a clue as to the whereabouts of the culprit. This was serious—we had at least two guns inside the secure area and no way to find the owner. I sounded the alarm, which stopped all screenings area to stop all activity. No one in, no one out—period. The magnitude of this breach began to settle in. Since all parts of the secured terminal are open to the passengers, once they are past the checkpoint, the culprit could be anywhere in the terminal. Sky Harbor International Airport Terminal 4's operations came to a halt. Starting with the last seat on every airplane loading during this time, every person was to be routed back out through their gate's checkpoint for rescreening. Of course, the new folks wanting to depart were held at the checkpoint. The massive chore of sterilizing the terminal was begun by having the maintenance staff assist the shop and venders owners collecting and removing all garbage from their areas. Possibly the weapons could be hidden among it to be retrieved later. All planes that had loaded and left during this time frame were directed to a secure location on the airport to be searched.

The herding of the passengers completed, which surprisingly met with little resistance. Seemed various stories of why the evacuation had spread only to our aid. The process was slow but meticulous. Estimates later were six thousand people were involved. One and a half hours later, all areas having been searched void of people, the call went out to start screening people again. All personnel were reminded to BOLO (be on the lookout) for the guns coming back through.

Fifteen minutes into the process, I was advised the guns had returned. Screener at terminal C had them. I hurried to that location to see two pistols in a backpack on the monitor.

To my joy a superior, screener, and a passenger were all there waiting my arrival. I couldn't hardly wait to see what was behind this huge cluster F.

The bag was bought out first to reveal two chrome-plated cap guns. Yep, full-sized cap guns. The story began to unfold. Our owner, an attractive female actress, explained she was on her way to California to audition for a part. The guns were part of her props. Since *she* knew they were harmless, she put them in her backpack. OMG, six thousand people inconvenienced, thousands of dollars wasted on outgoing connecting flights, delays and canceled meetings. Harmless, really. She was quite calm about her part and wouldn't be charged as she hadn't committed any crimes. Oh yes, she was a blonde. I never found out what happened to the runway screener, but the following day, I was summoned to the LT's office for what I assumed was an "Atta boy" for my overall stellar performance. Nope, he wanted to advise me the airport had a spokesman, and since I had talked to a reporter who published the incident on the front page the next day, the airport was pissed, thus so was he. Geeez.

You might be wondering about that invisible gun mentioned earlier. Another checkpoint story. Called to B Checkpoint on a weapon find. It had only been one minute since the call, so pretty quick response. Maybe I need to explain the FAA's rules regarding response to checkpoints. A major reason for our appearance at airports is the timely requirement to contact and seize any weapons trying to enter the secure areas. I.e., no weapons allowed. The staff at the checkpoints shouldn't be responsible for that duty. I saw the image of a small handgun in a suitcase on the monitor where I was met by a supervisor who seemed reluctant to talk. "Where's the weapon?" was met with "I'm not sure." *Oh no, here we go again. I just saw it.* "Where's the subject?"

Again, "I don't know."

Frustrated, I asked if she could point him out since only minutes had passed.

"I think so." Time's a-wasting, I ushered her into the secure area, and almost immediately, she pointed him out. I made contact, asking him to come with me back to the checkpoint. Puzzled, he complied. I noticed he was carrying a small suitcase similar to the image on the monitor we were now looking at.

"Is that your only carry-on luggage?" I motioned to his hand.

"Yes, sir, is there a problem?"

I pointed to the image on the screen, saying, "I'm told that's your bag."

"Sir, I don't even own a gun. That's not mine." Other officers had taken his bag and searched it, declaring no gun in it. Of course, yes, during this time, all checkpoints were shut down and backing up people.

Fed up with the evasiveness, I took the supervisor to the side and in my best police voice said, "Is or was there a gun in his bag?"

"No." What was going on here? But first things first. I advised radio, "No gun involved, open all checkpoints." I could almost hear the collective sigh of relief from my supervisors. The crisis over, now was the time to get to bottom of this mystery. The gentleman involved also wanted to know how a gun had gotten in his bag, or did it?

The supervisor explained she had recently received a gadget that allowed her to put false images on the screener's monitors. Pretty slick way to keep them on their toes, she thought. Earlier today, she had done just that and the test was successful. Some two hours later, this ghost image had appeared in our now slightly upset travelers. We tried to explain the necessity for security as he walked off, shaking his head. The operation was returning to normal when a call of a disturbance on B Concourse came out. Now what? That was close to our gun call. I was walking up to a small angry crowd when I saw our hapless traveler surrounded. I sent the band of vigilantes away and found that folks had thought he was responsible for the delays at the checkpoint. An airlines representative came to the rescue by buying him a new shirt and housing him in their preferred club.

My partner Jimmy retired right at twenty years, which left me with a decision to make. I had twenty-two years on and staying to twenty-five would increased my pension by 12½ percent about one thousand a month. You say, "A no-brainer, right?" Yeah, me too. Around this time, we went into increased security arrangements. Can you believe it? More overtime for the troops. I was rolling in dough, working all the long hours I could handle. One day off every other week. The FAA (government agency regulating air traffic and airports) had put all airports on high alert due to terrorist activities. Translation—don't even think about parking your car at the curb to wait for your arriving passengers. We attacked the "No Parking Enforcement" rule with gusto. When you came to the airport, you had to be prepared to circle till your arriving guests were on the curb with their luggage. Didn't we have fun with this "No Exceptions" rule?

Typical encounter—"Sir, you need to move your car. No parking allowed,"

"I'm not parking. I'm waiting for my wife, who will be out in one sec." Out comes my ticket book and a wave to the passing wrecker to hook this one. Might take less than one minute and "Mister, my wife will be right out" now was standing on the curb as his vehicle was fading into the distance. Fifty-dollar fine, fifty-dollar tow bill. Next! We had this procedure down to a science. The tow trucks, of which we kept two or three roaming continually, were equipped with a quick connect hook that only took seconds to attach. In spite of the signs and our presence, many people left their cars and went inside looking for their arrivals. We had instructed the tow trucks if they saw a ticket on the windshield, hook it. We ticketed and towed hundreds of cars in the first couple of weeks. Before you begin to hate me, if you were one of them who found a vacant spot where you left your car, try to understand what was really behind the action. We wanted any potential terrorists to realize leaving a bomb-filled car at the curb would only blow up out in our unoccupied storage lot. Oh boy, did we piss off a lot of folks. I had people refuse to get out of their car as it was being towed; add a citation for failure to obey a police offer. One guy tried to stand between his car and the tow truck. Bingo, another citation for the city. One young gal screamed the whole time I was writing out her "failure to obey" ticket, only shutting up when I pulled out my handcuffs and said, "Sign or go directly to jail. You will not pass go and collect your two hundred dollars, believe me." These encounters kept our supervisors busy with complaints for sure. There were no exceptions, so everyone got treated the same, including several state politicians and a few city mayors. The high-alert status remained in effect for a long time, and in fact, a form of it still exists today. Currently, the officers will indulge the occasional fool who thinks he can bullshit you till his parties came out. Sky Harbor did not have an incident of a real threat of a car bomb left at the curb, nor did any airport to my knowledge. So that means our vigilance worked, or there never was a threat in the first place! We worked many long hours, made lots of overtime pay, and my goal to fatten my pension to max was surging forward.

A side benefit was coming in contact with some famous folks. Former President George H. W. Bush and Barbara, Senator Bob Dole, Vice President Gore, President Ronald and Nancy Reagan, Senator John McCain, former prime minister Margaret Thatcher, to mention a few. Most were very nice people and always thankful for our help in their protection.

My days were numbered, and I was seeing that light at the end of the tunnel racing at me. I completed my twenty-fifth year on November 18, 2000, and chose January 25, 2001, as my final working day. I only had to put in my time till then. I was "Put a fork in me" done. Listening to grown adults bitch and moan about petty issues does take a toll on you. I didn't want any more of it. On the appointed day, we had a nice retirement party at the airport with my wife Grace at my side, many old friends and family members attending. I got the usual ribbing, wonderful trophies, and many kind and thoughtful things were said about me. That day was kind of a blur, and too soon, I was walking away from twenty-five plus years on my dream job.

Many years later after retiring, I was contacted by a prosecutor in Oklahoma regarding one of my old cases. The call had me rewinding my mental tapes.

Rushed to a stabbing at the Seventh Avenue liquors had just occurred. Actually, I took my time since this was a biweekly event at that location. Cheapest boost in Phoenix with a great selection of Mad Dog's twenty-twenty wine. Mad Dog being one step down from Boone's Farm was the choice of our wino population.

Found a small gathering of Indians quite agitated, standing around a large brave lying on the ground. He had been stabbed in the chest and was bleeding. Three different groups knew what had happened, the suspect, and which way they went. Great we'll solve this quickly. Of course, when questioned, they really weren't even present for the crime. Fire rescue arrived and had to fight with the victim, who now was all puffed up, "I'm gonna kick the f——er's ass." I had found an actual witness and broadcast a suspect description. The victim had collapsed again and was being prepared for transport. Off he went with the siren blaring and red lights flashing. A unit a few blocks away advised of a subject matching my broadcast description was in custody. Headed that way to secure this person. Figured without my witness, who had refused to get involved any further, I'd have to do some detective work. This subject who had been found with a bloodstained knife on him was claiming innocence.

"I'm an Indian, I could never stab another Indian." Well, no one had told him there had been a stabbing. Good enough—he matched the description, had the weapon on him, and knew the essence of the crime.

"Book 'um, Danno." I learned later the victim's alcohol-infused body died on the operating table. The detectives changed the charges to murder.

Now back to current affairs.

Seemed our Indian suspect had murdered two Indian people in the northern part of the state of Oklahoma. He had been found guilty and was awaiting the death penalty phase of his trial. Enter me and the suspect's statement: "I'm an Indian, I could never stab another Indian." He had made the exact same claim to his arresting officer in his current situation. His statement was to be used as a part of the state's request for the death penalty. I was off to Oklahoma on a jet and hooked up with the investigating officer. Arriving at the prosecutor's office, I thought the building looked familiar. It was the Court House where Timothy McVay was shown being removed by marshals following the Oklahoma City bombing.

The prosecutor needed me to testify about the statement his Indian defendant had made back in Phoenix. It would show aggravating circumstances or such. He also wondered how this convicted murderer had been released after serving only fifteen months. I told him I couldn't help him with travesties of justice.

I waited outside on a wooden bench in this Sooner State's Courthouse. I had dressed for the occasion in my western suit, complete with my vest and Stetson. I'm told I clean up nice.

"Officer Fribbs!" called the bailiff. "Please enter the courtroom." I ambled in and up to the witness chair. Glancing at the jury, I gave them a little western nod. What a ham I can be. The prosecutor went through his spiel, introducing me to the panel.

He had me explain my involvement with the defendant. He asked if the suspect had made any statements regarding his role in the crime. "Yes," was my response as I watched the jury lean forward. I spoke his utterances word for word while watching their reactions.

A young girl juror in the front row smiled at me and muttered to herself, "I knew it." My cameo appearance over, I was ushered back out to my pew.

I left the next day and soon learned our liar was off to Old Sparky or whatever they use for executions in Oklahoma.

If you are considering a career in law enforcement, realize once committed, you will never be the same person again. The things you'll do, see, and experience are like nothing else in any other occupation.

That said, "Increase your weight training, hit those books, do 10Ks, and take that next entrance exam."

Ride on, trooper—the beat goes on!

Night Fire

Dedication

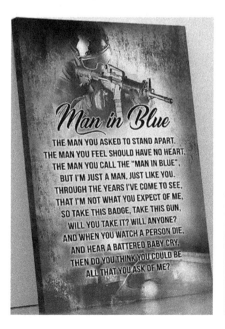

ABOUT THE AUTHOR

He was born in Ottawa, Illinois where following High School graduation he attended Black Hawk College receiving his Associate Degree. He is retired from the City of Phoenix Police Department after serving as an Officer from 1975 to 2001. He is married to his wife Grace of 32 years and they share five children and nine grandchildren. Tom and Grace enjoy traveling while residing half the year in Flagstaff, Arizona and the other half in Maui, Hawaii.

CPSIA information can be obtained
at www.ICGtesting.com
Printed in the USA
FFHW021831051218
49764094-54237FF